F. COMENCINI '99

Clara Vada Padovani

nutella®
passion

**GREAT CHEFS AND CONFECTIONERS
SHARE THEIR PASSION
AND RECIPES FOR NUTELLA**

with a contribution by Gigi Padovani

and a preface by Andrea Lee

Texts:
Clara Vada Padovani pp. 8-11, 79-240, and Gigi Padovani pp. 22-77
Thanks go to Andrea Lee for the text of *Belle de Jour* pp. 16-19
and to Sabrina Notarnicola for the revision of the recipe texts

Translation:
Susanna Selmin (pp. 8-205), Betsy Burke for NTL (pp. 206-231)

English editing:
Anthony Brierley

Recipe consultant:
Francine Segan

Original photographs for the recipes:
Francesca Brambilla and Serena Serrani pp. 73, 83-157, and Marco Favi pp. 165-203
(unless otherwise stated in the iconographic references)

Image processing:
Serena Serrani

Home economists:
chef Federico Coria pp. 83-157 (except where realized by the recipe's creator)
Rosalba Gioffré pp. 165-203

Graphic design and cover:
Yoshihito Furuya

Layout:
Giovanni Mattioli

Editor:
Giada Riondino

Photo retouching:
Nicola Dini

Managing editor:
Davide Mazzanti

Thanks for the use of materials for the series of recipes on pp.165-203 go to:
Ceramiche Virginia, Montespertoli (FI), info@showroomvirginia.it
Franco Spini, Gifts, Wedding lists, Household items, Florence.

www.giunti.it

© 2010 Giunti Editore S.p.A.
via Bolognese 165 - 50139 Firenze - Italia
via Dante 4 - 20121 Milano - Italia

First edition: November 2010

Reprint	Year
4 3 2 1 0	2013 2012 2011 2010

Printed by Giunti Industrie Grafiche S.p.A. - Prato

«The discovery of a new dish confers
more happiness on humanity than
the discovery of a new star»
Anthelme Brillat-Savarin

To my mother Olga,
who dreamed of America

SWEET
EQUATIONS by Clara Vada Padovani

I remember that on the cardboard tray of pastries my father brought home on Sunday morning, there would always be one beignet left over. It was not polite to eat it. But, maybe, it was the best one. Desserts have an unfortunate destiny. They always arrive late, at the end of a meal. And so, especially if the menu isn't very well-balanced, many forgo it because they are already burdened by earlier calories, and they therefore miss out on a bit of happiness.

I'm not a particularly greedy person, but ever since I was old enough to putter around in the kitchen, flicking through the pages of cook books, I've been fatally attracted to cakes and biscuits, puddings and ice-creams. I've been buying cook books and magazines for the past twenty years. I collect recipes and copy them by hand into my exercise books. And looking through them, I realize that I've collected mostly notes and memories with a high sugar content.

It's true, I love the "d side" of life and of cooking, connected to sweet things: beating eggs, sugar... whipping cream, egg whites... kneading flour... having the house scented with the inebriating perfume of freshly toasted hazelnuts and almonds, looking at the magic of leavening through the glass door of the oven, taking a pudding out of the fridge and turning it out perfectly onto a plate... and the ultimate pleasure of seeing the joy in the eyes of my guests.

The passion of a *gourmet* or the desire of a *gourmand*? Maybe both.

Perhaps to compensate for the dryness of the numbers which have accompanied me for most of my life, forging in me a certain severity towards myself.

Perhaps to overcome moments of professional depression, due to the less than satisfactory results of some of my students, the arrogant ones convinced that «math isn't useful, all you need is a calculator, not even that, we've got cell phones ...». And I would spend a few patient months struggling to make them appreciate this subject and even find it enjoyable.

Perhaps to suppress those inevitable feelings of guilt which assault every working mother-taxi driver-party organizer, I would reward myself on Saturday afternoon by preparing cakes and pastries for my daughter Alice and her friends.

Maybe... no, surely, I took refuge in making desserts because my "forma mentis" frame of mind has always made me appreciate a characteristic element of sweet recipes: their scientific precision. In savory cooking you can remedy a small mistake but not in pastry cooking. No, you have to start from scratch, just like a mathematical equation.

I love perfection, when humanly possible, but I also love simplicity. Therefore I've always avoided preparations that take too long, or with ingredients which are too hard to find or recipes complicated by the use of too many technical tools. My culinary creations are born from the temptation to vary or substitute an ingredient, like the recipes with Nutella which I recommend in this book.

Why Nutella?

Perhaps because, as a little girl, I was only given Nutella as a prize, after having been "good" and so, since it was so rare at home, it was the best afternoon snack ever, at my school friends' homes.

Perhaps because it was the symbol of an unforgettable complicity with my grandmother Caterina, notoriously greedy and always ready to grant my every wish, and the memory of the family hazelnut grove in the Langa region, with my summers, still a teenager, spent helping to harvest the nuts that would be sent to the Ferrero factory.

Maybe for all those occasions when I managed to let my students taste the sweetness of math by organizing a Nutella party at school when everyone in class got a good vote in a test. Maybe, or rather, surely, because it represents my youth, my generation, the strong attachment I have with my native land, and the city where I used to breathe in the Nutella air that poured out of the chimneys of the largest chocolate factory in Europe.

In this book I've gathered together all my sweet satisfactions, dividing them into the various moments of the day: breakfast, children's afternoon snacks, tea-time and dinner with friends. They are simple suggestions, easily made, with ingredients that can be found in most stores and supermarkets. These recipes reflect my personality, my vision of "dietetically correct" culinary art, eliminating or reducing the amount of sugar, butter and fat in general, compared to the original recipe, and using a "modest amount" of Nutella to give a touch of delight, color and taste.

I love to eat for pleasure, to travel around Italy looking for special products and extraordinary restaurants, getting to know the personality and the genius of a chef or a pastry cook. Therefore, it has been exciting for me to eat a parfait, first with just an orange sauce and then perfected "live" with the tartness of tomato jelly. It has been surprising to taste a wafer of foie gras and Nutella or have the gustatory explosion of an unrepeatable hazelnut come forth.

In his play *Vera; or, the Nihilists,* Oscar Wilde has one of the characters say: «You are wrong to run down cookery. For myself, the only immortality I desire is to invent a new sauce». I personally don't know if the inventor of Nutella will ever become immortal, or just simply win the Nobel Prize, as has already been proposed by the television anchorman, Fabio Fazio, but certainly my cook and pastry chef friends, who enthusiastically and with a pinch of self-irony accepted my invitation to be inspired by this legendary spreading cream, will achieve eternal glory in the "Dante's circle" of worldwide Nutella addicts. Their greatest satisfaction, in Italy as in New York, has been looking at my face as I tasted their recipe for the first time, that special recipe created to give a touch of unpredictability and great professionalism to this book.

I'm aware that this is just "another" cook book, and that there are many others. But it is also unique. Because for the first time famous and prestigious chefs and pastry-cooks, all awarded the many hats and stars of the best gastronomical guides, have playfully used this product, Nutella, which represents such a strong image in our collective memory. A hazelnut spread so well known that it needs no further publicity. It's become the playful "glue" between two parallel worlds: that of cooking and that of pastry making.

In truth, I like to believe that this book might represent something more, that it may put some of the most prestigious young artists of the new Italian cuisine more in the limelight. In fact, in addition to the already excellent team that gathered for the first edition of *Nutella Passion*, this time we have female chefs and other young cooks of

the *Bel Paese*, this beautiful Italy, as well as some leading protagonists of the coolest restaurants in New York, inspired by the "made in Italy" tradition. The bond which they share and which unites them, across the two shores of the ocean, is the constant quest for typical prime materials and products. They are cooks and pastry chefs obviously not used to using supermarket food in their recipes, but they are tied to our land, our variegated Italy.

Nutella is an emblem of Italian innovation and creativity. It is one of the best known Italian trademarks in the world and it deserves this tribute. A spreading cream born from our chocolate-making tradition, with the hazelnuts of the Langhe, my home land: an industrial product that has become, with time, a legend.

Clara Vada Padovani

CONTENTS

Nutella passion | Sweet Equations

BELLE
DE JOUR by Andrea Lee

I certainly never consciously aspired to the dubious status of international pundit on the Cult of Nutella. However the fact is that over a decade ago, for fun, I wrote for «The New Yorker» a short humorous piece on Nutella that alerted the ever-ravenous American public to the existence of the fabled Italian hazelnut spread. From the privileged vantage point of an American writer living in Europe, I spoke of the curious passion for an unctuous mixture of cocoa and hazelnuts, that in Italy, unites old and young, avant-garde city intellectuals and traditionalist villagers, right-and left-wing politicians in a near-orgasmic haze of well-being. With tongue firmly in cheek, I deconstructed Nutella in terms of politics, of philosophy, of sex and other basic instincts. I hinted at global trends. But what I did not reveal was my own personal relationship with Nutella, which began years earlier in a kitchen, one hot summer afternoon in Rome.

Imagine a young American woman freshly arrived in the Eternal City from the United States, world headquarters of what we shall euphemistically call leisure food. In Rome, she is captivated by the wonders of "carciofi alla Giudea", and "spaghetti alla carbonara"; yet, at the same time, she misses purely frivolous American food like nacho chips and brownies. On this momentous afternoon, she stands staring into a small, open jar with a red and white label. Her thoughts run: «How strange to spread chocolate on bread... On television, they say it's healthy... Children love it... Lots of sugar, probably... Not like peanut butter at all... What exactly are hazelnuts? And the name, how odd and retro. Nutella.... Like Cinderella. Noo-tell-a. Or like something out of Nabokov. Lo-li-ta... Nu-tell-a...». Meditatively she dips the tip of her right index finger into the jar, and brings a taste of chocolate cream to her tongue. And so, in the same instant it took Pandora to unlatch a box, or Eve to bite into a nameless fruit, begins a lifelong passion. The flavor and the mysteriously enveloping texture, a glutinous, not-quite-bland mixture of sugar and cocoa, are strange to her, one of the many new gustatory experiences she has had in Italy. Yet there is also something hauntingly familiar about it, as if she has known it all her life. Late that night she will get up and eat Nutella again. This time with a spoon.

Reader, I was that young woman, and through all the turns and twists of an expatriate writer's life: marriage, books, birth of children, more books, travels, divorce; remarriage – Nutella was always somehow present. T.S. Eliot's Prufrock, poor man, is said to have measured out his life in coffee spoons, but I confess that my life abroad might be measured out in Nutella jars.

My bilingual children, born in Italy, grew up eating grilled Nutella sandwiches after school; a favorite anecdote is how my daughter dropped a two kilo jar of Nutella on the floor – the sound of it breaking is KLOOMP. My Italian husband invented a new verb: Nutellare. To Nutella. When we travelled around the world on vacation, we usually took a jar of Nutella with us, especially to America. But, as if my New Yorker article had been prophecy, as the new century wore on, we began to find it in out-of-the-way places: Hong Kong; Kenya; Madagascar. My fifteen year old son reported this year from his boarding school near Boston that girls – American girls – bring Nutella from their rooms to breakfast. Globalization is now a reality for Nutella, and what does that mean? It means that there was a niche in the world ready for comfort that is not provided by a fizzy drink in a can, or a set of golden arches. It means that Italy, whose indefatigable explorers shaped the history of the expanding world, has made one more step in the tango of cultural influences that move back and forth across the Atlantic. The gist of it is that the Americas once sent chocolate to Europe, and now Europe is returning the favor. With hazelnuts.

Nowadays, Ferrero's Canadian factory is up and running, and the stage is set for the last act of the Nutella drama: the conquest of North America. Even in an age of fear over supersizing, its success seems a foregone conclusion. Americans, like Italians, will be captivated not just by the enveloping chocolate flavor of Nutella, but by the charm of its quirky two-faced image. One of the first things one notes when inquiring into the cult of Nutella is the enticing contrast between its wholesome family advertising, and the open secret that something so delicious is secretly naughty. In fact, it is the "belle de jour" of European family foods.

Part of Nutella spread's double-faced appeal lies in the fact that it is both traditionally Italian – hazelnut chocolate creams called "gianduja" have a long history in the Piedmont region of Italy – yet at the same time is a definitive mass-produced product of the postwar era whose basic culture was determined by America. The name Nutella, for example, is a play on two English words, with an appealingly retro trace of the twentieth century American mania for attention-grabbing commercial names. It already sounds like an American product. And the irresistible concept of gooey nut butter and chocolate to spread on bread is so suited to the American snack food culture that one wonders why it didn't already exist – in the land of peanut butter and jelly, and fried Twinkies, and marshmallow fluff. In the end, the advent of Nutella in the United States is somewhat of a spiritual homecoming.

As for my own relationship with Nutella: over the years, it has evolved into something like the sort of arrangement a nineteenth-century gentleman might have with a long-beloved mistress. Sometimes we breakfast together. Sometimes we are intimate at odd times of the day, and sometimes we don't encounter each other for weeks on end. Sometimes, exasperated with overindulgence, I ban Nutella from my house. And at other times the old passion flares up, and I will find myself, after midnight, in my kitchen with an open jar and a spoon in hand. Nu-tell-a. It is in fact a Lolita-like blend of childish delight and adult temptation. It is, like Nabokov's classic novel, a celebration of European and American influences, of high and low culture. So raise your knives and your spoons in celebration, O schoolchildren and housewives, and chefs, and sensualists at large. Your pleasure, and mine, is now spread all over the world.

Andrea Lee

NOCTURNAL INTERIORS

by Gigi Padovani

Silence. The room is lit only by the glow of a computer.

Oscar Wilde wrote that good things either harm you or are off limits. This is an exception. The jar is full. As I turn the lid I realize that it's never been opened. I go on. I turn the lid in a 360° swirl, slowly, knowingly. Then there's a snag, a hitch. I've reached the point of no return. If I go on, I'll have to admit to opening the jar. But the real obstacle has yet to come. It's the inner, golden seal that covers the round opening over the jar.

Breaking through that protective seal is the real beginning of the ritual. It has to be a slow movement, so as not to make any noise, but it has to be sharp enough to rip it open. And immediately you sense the inimitable scent. The sensation of hazelnuts, persistent. Of oil, of vanilla and of sugar. Then before you know it, the scent of cocoa is in your nostrils.

Your mouth fills with moisture, your brain is already imagining the melting cream on your tongue. The spoon sinks softly. The violated surface wrinkles, there's a small movement in the cream, it gives way, it shapes itself around the spoon, it penetrates without hesitation.

I lift the spoon and under it filaments of cream lengthen as I pull away. The scent goes straight to my brain. I'm intoxicated. The first spoonful is deep, sinful but quick. The

cream sticks immediately to the lips, then it seeps onto the tongue, it ends up at the back of my palate, softly insinuating itself between my teeth. I stop, enraptured.

One spoonful is not enough. It's only the beginning. My mouth wants more, more cocoa, more hazelnuts, more sugar. The pleasurable sensation starts to flow through my body. I don't tire of it. I have to think, feel, the flavor, the way I've been taught in tasting classes. Here comes the aftertaste. Hazelnuts, vanilla, cocoa. But there's another feeling. What's this new sensation? A 1960's kitchen with a yellowing Formica table and chairs with tubular stainless steel legs. Small rubber feet. I'm about to go to school, High school. An open jar on the table. A breakfast cup of white milk. A slice of bread. On the record player a Patty Pravo song is playing. In the hall my Latin and ancient Greek books are waiting, tied together by a green rubber band.

The wave of memories overwhelms me for a second. Maybe I'm exaggerating, but I plunge the spoon again. A slightly salty aftertaste now. A sip of cold water. I go to look for a CD with the music by the Piper Club girl! What kind of world would it be without Nutella?

[from *Gnam, Storia sociale della Nutella*, 1999, Roma]

Gigi Padovani

SOME LIKE IT SPREAD

The origins in the hazelnuts of the Langhe This hazelnut spread, now famous all over the world, could only have been created at Alba, a small town in Piedmont lying in the midst of undulating hills that rise and roll like sea waves. If the ridges of the Bassa Langa hills are cloaked with vines that produce some of the most famous wines in Italy – Barolo, Barbaresco, Dolcetto – on higher ground, where the peaks are covered in woods and gorges, hazelnut groves flourish and regale us with harvests of an oily fruit whose unmistakable aroma softens the bitterness of cocoa. The nut has a special name. It is the *tonda e gentile del Piemonte*, the delicate round hazelnut of the Piedmont region, named and prized for its shape and flavor. And ever since the middle of the eighteenth century the Turin chocolate-makers have been creating a soft tempting chocolate: the *gianduiotto*.

In this peaceful little town in the Langhe region, sixty kilometers south of Turin, after the end of the Second World War the creation of Nutella's forerunner was taking place. The confectioner who invented it was Pietro Ferrero (1898-1949), and he called the foil-wrapped sweet bar «Giandujot». It was meant to be sliced and was made with hazelnuts (easily found locally and cheap), sugar, a little cocoa and vegetable oils. The hungry children of post-war Italy began eating the new delight on slices of bread and were immediately won over. This, the original product, made between the end of 1945 and the beginning of 1946, was the "idea" that made possible the rapid growth of an industrial fortune that has no equal in Italian business history.

In the space of just three generations the Ferrero dynasty went from being a shop in the winding lanes of the old town of Alba to a multinational company that is one of the world's leaders in the confectionery sector, with an annual turnover (2008-2009) of 6.3 billion euros, 21 thousand employees, 18 manufacturing plants in five continents and a yearly production of more than one million tons of product, from pralines, breath mints and the famous double chocolate eggs, to school snacks, cold teas and frozen desserts. Every idea unique and inimitable, and yet all inspired by the classics of the confectionery and pastry-making tradition: this was the philosophy of

Left: from the very start Ferrero acquired a fleet of trucks to distribute their products.
Center: the Giandujot is Nutella's precursor, a hazelnut and cocoa bar made to be cut into slices.

Right: Ferrero's very first illustrated advertisement dating from just after the war.
The company started in Alba, a town in southern Piedmont. In the photo, Piazza Risorgimento.

Nutella passion | Some like it Spread

Pietro's son, Michele Ferrero, and one which he has instilled into the company ever since he took over at the age of twenty-four, with his mother Piera Cillario, when his father suddenly died in 1949.

If Pietro, the "scientist" of the family, was the inventor of a specialty that transformed the simple eating habits of Italian children, it was his brother Giovanni, seven years younger, who guaranteed its success. Marketing and commerce were his passion and with his red Fiat 1100 he plied the country roads of northern Italy, selling Ferrero sweets directly to small shops in tiny towns, bypassing the wholesalers. In 1947 there were 12 company vans with the motto «Sono stato il primo e resto il migliore» (I was the first and I'm still the best); by 1954 they numbered 154, in 1955 they had increased to 804, and in the 1960s, 2000: a fleet of cars equal in number to that of the Italian Army. Those small yellow vans with chocolate-colored stripes made millions of children happy.

Like the pioneers of American chocolate, Milton Hershey and Forrest Mars, the Swiss confectioners Rudolph Lindt and Henry Nestlé, the Englishman John Cadbury and the Dutchman Conrad van Houten, Pietro Ferrero and his son Michele were "self made men" who helped transform post-war Italy into an industrial power. Their contribution to the economic growth of the country was important and decisive, wrote the journalist Domenico Bartoli in his book *Storia di un successo*, published in 1967. The Ferrero group has remained a family enterprise, now headed by two CEO's, Giovanni and Pietro, sons of Michele who have never sought allies in the stock market, and who have kept the company firmly in the founding family's hands.

Left: the forerunners of Nutella: Cremalba, and Supercrema, which was sold from 1949 in large 1 pound jars.

Right: one of the advertising calendars made by the Alba company which were distributed to their retailers. The Ferrero trademark was changed in 1964.

On the 20th of April 1964 a star was born   The sliceable Giandujot very soon became a spread. It was proudly named "Supercrema" and was sold in ½-kilo glass jars or in saucepans that housewives could re-use. But how did it become a cream?

Like many other sweets, from Savoyard biscuits to panettone, the origins of the spread are shrouded in mystery. Perhaps one of those Giandujot bars melted on a hot summer day in 1949.

Michele Ferrero had guessed that the hazelnut cream would be fantastic to spread on bread. But after the first step, another was necessary. A name that would change the "ugly duckling" into a beautiful swan and make it legendary.

New names were studied: Cremalba, Nussy, Tartinoise in France. To conquer the European markets, a brand name was needed, one that would make people forget about the little town in Piedmont.

The Mexican intellectual Carlos Fuentes commented that writers have to be able to "name" the world with an ethical use of words. This was true for Nutella. The attractive naming, which sounded like a vocal caress, successfully determined a fame which never faded. An "evergreen" that defied the marketing theory regarding the life span of a product, which calculates that after a peak in sales a decline is inevitable.

Even the lettering, the choice of the print characters used to identify the logo, contributed to making Nutella a legend, and today that logo is worth hundreds of millions of Euros.

In this case *nomina sunt consequentia rerum*, as the Roman emperor Justinian I of Byzantium wrote. In fact, since the name Supercrema could no longer be used due to a law of 1963, the Ferrero managers were forced to think up a new name. What should they call it? Nussina, Nutina, Nusscrem?

Left: a jar of Supercrema in a television advertisement, just before the launch of Nutella in 1964: the selling points were always the hazelnuts and a slice of bread.

Right: the first advertising campaign designed by Studio Stile of Milan, with the prototypes drawn up by Lelo Cremonesi and Gian Rossetti.

The winning idea came to Michele Ferrero at the end of 1963 when he was in Germany and the company's local managers, including Severino Chiesa, were called upon to decide on a new name in a hurry. «It will be Nutella», Michele Ferrero told his wife, Maria Franca, his close collaborator in the company. «It will remind everyone that it's made from hazelnuts».

The launch of the new product was preceded by a testing phase, assigned to the first guru of marketing and consumer trends, Giampaolo Fabris (1938-2010), who recounted his experience as follows (from the preface of *Gnam*): «I was just twenty years old when I was appointed by the company to test the new name chosen to re-launch Supercrema in Europe. It was my first working experience. At that time the absolute *deus ex machina* of the confectionery enterprise, founded by his father Pietro, was Michele Ferrero, a man of extraordinary openness, a genius who understood before other multinationals the importance of the "impossible to clone" rule. We carefully researched how the logo would be received by consumers in Germany, France and England. It was one of the very first marketing operations in Italy. The launching campaign for the product was designed by a Milanese graphic studio and started with the distribution of posters showing a slice of bread spread with Nutella. The image of chocolate was thus reclaimed in Italy: no longer just a bar of dark chocolate but a smooth cream to spread on a slice of bread. Bread that is reassuring, homemade, protective, maternal. It has the same significance that milk has in other Ferrero products, with the famous slogan, "more milk, less cocoa". It was an intelligent move, since the relationship Italians had with chocolate was ambivalent. It was generally regarded as a luxury food for special occasions, and even rather unhealthy, especially for children».

The graphic studio mentioned by Fabris was Studio Stile. Its owners, in the Sixties, were Lele Cremonesi and Gian

Left: the cartoon series *Il Gigante Amico* was broadcast on television from 1971 to 1976 in the programme *Carosello*. The scripts were written by Romano Bertola. The wicked hawk Jo Condor gets up to a lot of mischief but is always defeated by the friendly giant.

Rossetti, the artist who had designed the famous slice of bread represented in the early advertisements. On 17 March 1964 the patent was registered and the production of the Nutella jars started in the Alba factory on 26 April 1964. A historical date for the company, for on the very same day the United States and Russia announced the first reduction of their atomic plans.

That year was full of changes, for customs and culture: Andy Warhol and Roy Lichtenstein brought Pop Art to the Venice Biennial exhibition; Mary Quant launched the mini-skirt; Betty Friedan introduced the feminist movement to America and Twiggy appeared on just about every magazine cover.

Nutella arrived a year later in France and Germany, in Australia only in 1978 (the Lithgow factory near Sydney), while the United States had to wait until 1985. In 2006 Nutella production for the NAFTA area was moved from Somerset in New Jersey to Brantford in Canada, not far from Toronto.

The largest Nutella factory in the world, however, is the one at Alba, where every day dozens of trucks deliver 140 tons of hazelnuts and a merry-go-round of automatic nipples unendingly fills glass jars with the creamy spread. Another Italian Nutella production center is at Sant'Angelo dei Lombardi (Avellino).

Also impressive is the French Ferrero factory at Viller-Ecalles, in Normandy, and the German factory of Stadtallendorf, a few miles from Frankfurt. In 1992 Nutella production started at Belsk Duzy, 40 kilometers south of Warsaw, and the last country to start production was Brazil in 2005, with the factory at Pocos de Caldas.

Nutella represents roughly 17% of the global turnover of the Ferrero Group (compared to the 24% of chocolates and the 16% of eggs). If all the jars produced in the world in one year were placed side by side, around the world, the row would be 1.3 times that of the globe's circumference, in other words some 50 thousand kilometers.

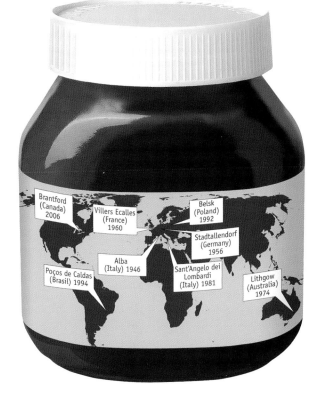

FERRERO

Lo sapevi che?

La fila dei vasetti di Nutella prodotti in un anno è lunga 1,3 volte la circonferenza della terra.

Nutella passion | Some like it Spread

Les crêpes de **nutella**®

Above: Nutella is produced worldwide in eight different manufacturing plants. The first to open was the one at Alba in 1946, followed by the German and French factories. The Ferrero cream then "spread" to other continents: Australia, South America and Canada, the latter the location of the most recently established major plant.

Upper right: each year a row of Nutella jars is produced that exceeds the length of the Earth's 40 thousand kilometer circumference.

Right: advertisement in France where crêpes and Nutella, often sold in kiosks on the street, are a popular combination.

In the homes of millions of families you drink from glasses in which Nutella has been sold: a great promotional gimmick. The initial series with geometric designs was followed by those with cartoons, like Looney Tunes, and The Smurfs. Collectors search for the rarer series: like those dedicated to Nutella Parties, the zodiac signs, the Pink Panther and the "Coccodritti", the crocodiles of the Kinder surprises.

Nutella passion | Some like it Spread

Bread and glasses

Almost all over the world Nutella glasses have become collectors' items, memories of childhood, or just plain kitchen glasses. In Italy a mania for these everyday glass objects started up immediately; after drinking glasses came carafes, jars, bottles, and beer mugs. In 1964 the first drinking glass was called Kristal.

Then came hundreds of shapes and thousands of designs. The 1990s witnessed the start of series inspired by the characters of children's cartoons; from Walt Disney classics to those of Warner Bros., like Sylvester the Cat, Asterix in France, the Smurfs and heroes like Wonder Woman and Superman.

Not to mention European football stars, zodiac signs and Italian first names, etc. All these series are today highly sought after by collectors, who, like Luca Curati from Milan, possibly the most important collector in Italy, exchange information through printed or on-line catalogs and organize auctions on e-bay or enthusiasts' sites.

Over the years the devotion that Nutella has generated among its fans has extended to the drinking glasses which have become an icon of convivial pleasure.

Particularly at the end of the 1990s Ferrero represented Nutella as a cult commodity, using publicity campaigns that were emotionally inspiring. It then returned to more rational themes, based on the recommended daily use of a nourishing product. Ever since the 1960s, in every Italian magazine, the Ferrero cream has been presented as a «delight to spread on bread». «Nutella is a ration of the healthiest ingredients offered up by nature: sugar, hazelnuts, milk and the taste of cocoa. Spread on a slice of bread, an excellent breakfast that's cheering and heartwarming for all», was the slogan written under a photograph of the model family, the father in jacket and tie and the children, smiling and spruce, ready for a day at school.

Facing page: it is 1975, the year that saw the launching of a series of television advertisements with the catch-phrase «*Mamma tu lo sai*» («Mommy, you know»), reminding mothers that the same product they ate as children is now the ideal breakfast for their own children because it is trustworthy and nutritious. The production was commissioned to Pubbliregia, a Pino Torinese based agency that was part of the Ferrero group.

Right: the decision to focus on breakfast – «a delicious cream to spread on bread» – was made by Ferrero in 1964, as shown in this advertisement that appeared in magazines of the time.

Whether it's a sinful pleasure of the palate or a healthy morning habit (providing about 350 calories, primarily carbohydrates, if spread on a slice of bread and eaten with a glass of milk: a combination suggested by many dieticians), Nutella has accompanied the daily life of Europeans for decades. It's hard to resist.

The message in the jar   According to Jean Baudrillard, the world of objects «has something to say, in that each of them goes far beyond its pure and simple use», especially if it has entered the «world of signs» as frequently happens with successful products. Signs or dreams? In a society dominated by the ecstasy of communication, as the French sociologist would say, everything becomes the «dream of the products». And when a product becomes a cult brand, like Nutella, even normal images become inadequate. It is not easy to represent the magic world now associated with the word Nutella. In fact, it has become synonymous not only with a hazelnut spread but also with a «sinful cream», the «holy grail of greed», «a Proustian madeleine», «socializing insofar as unique», «a contemporary fetish», «the jar of desire». A concentrate of culture, the passion of top models and sporting idols, the inspiring muse for books, films, paintings and operas.

One of the most well-known Italian brands in the world, as famous if not more famous than Ferrari, Nutella would now need a language of its own, like Esperanto, to be interpreted, for existing idioms are simply not enough. The sweetness represented by that jar is like a cheerful babble of languages, lit up by the aura of a legend fuelled by internet sites, newspapers, songs, books and sports champions. French kids love it, served inside a warm crêpe. Whole generations of Germans plunge their spoons into the jar, ready to start a new day with the taste of Gianduia cream.

Advertising campaigns the world over have always laid emphasis on the consumption of Nutella within the family. An important role is played by the parents: a father or mother is shown next to a child who is seen growing up eating hazelnut cream spread on a piece of bread.

Among the most "addicted", besides the Italians, are the Belgians, chocolate lovers almost by definition, and the French, who boast a consumption of 1 kilo per person per year. Italy is still family-based: three out of four families have a jar at home, 50% more than the French or the Germans.

The modernness of Nutella lies not, however, in its planetary success. This happens to many industrial products in the age of globalization. The question is, how is it possible for a hazelnut and cocoa cream to generate such a mass reaction, from generation to generation, and now "spread" its way from the heart of Europe to the rest of the world? One of the secrets is undoubtedly the integrity of the image that has survived intact over time: the shape of the jar, the label, the name and the lettering of the logo have all been identical from the very start and are distinctly characteristic of the product.

The Canadian writer Marshall McLuhan, in his book *Understanding Media: The Extensions of Man*, which made him famous throughout the world as the first expert on modern means of mass communication, claimed that the media are an extension of man's senses, regardless of whether or not they have any definable "content". From this analysis comes his famous assertion – «the medium is the message» – with which he starts his book.

Since McLuhan was convinced that the prime materials of a community are jointly goods and media, we could apply this same theory to Nutella. A generational symbol, a vehicle for society's values, an image that conveys other concepts, the hazelnut cream jar has, yes, used all media, especially television, to spread its message throughout the world, but in turn has also been used by the media to pass on other messages and values.

Tag für Tag: „guten Morgen Nutella"

Was gesunde, muntere Kinder so an einem Tag laufen, springen, kraxeln und turnen . . . aber auch denken und Neues erfassen, ist wirklich erstaunlich.

Ernährungsbewußte Mütter bieten daher ihren Kindern täglich das grundgesunde Nutella-Frühstück. Das ergiebige Glas reicht für eine lange Reihe köstlicher Nutella-Brote.

Nutella schenkt mit seinem Reichtum an lebenswichtigen Eiweißstoffen aus Milch und in südlicher Sonne gereiften Haselnüssen Energie und Ausdauer für den ganzen Tag. Für heute. Für morgen. Für übermorgen . . .

Daß Nutella mit seinem delikaten Haselnußgeschmack Kindern ganz besonders gut schmeckt, macht es der sorgenden Mutter nur zusätzlich leichter.

Also ab heute: „Guten Morgen, Nutella . . ."

Nutella enthält Proteine, Spurenelemente, Kalzium usw.

für heute – für morgen – für übermorgen

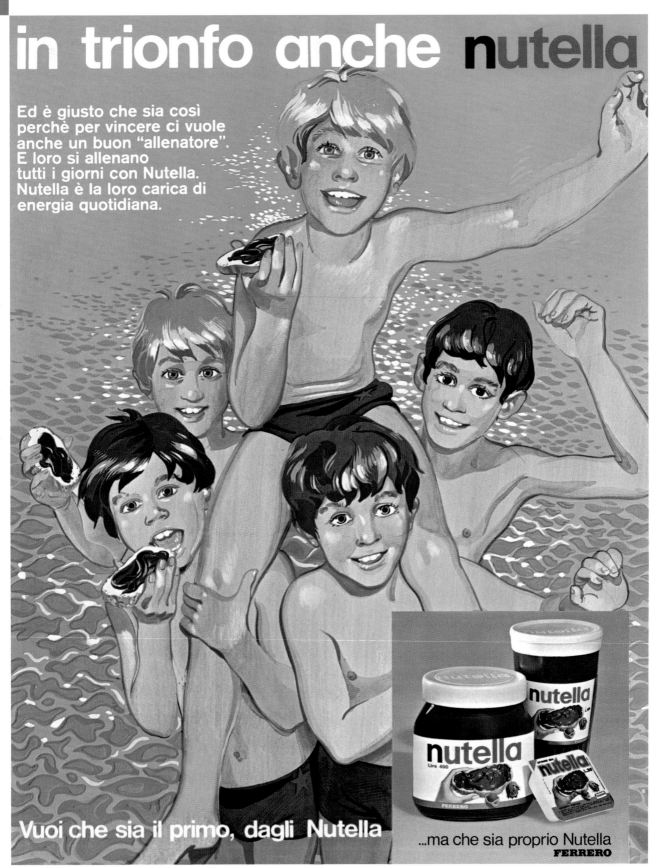

in trionfo anche nutella

Ed è giusto che sia così
perchè per vincere ci vuole
anche un buon "allenatore".
E loro si allenano
tutti i giorni con Nutella.
Nutella è la loro carica di
energia quotidiana.

Vuoi che sia il primo, dagli Nutella

...ma che sia proprio Nutella

FERRERO

Facing page: the energy contained in a jar of Nutella is recommended for people who do sports. During the Seventies and Eighties many publicity campaigns developed this concept in printed and televised advertising, not only in Italy.

Now a well-known product worldwide, children have learnt to say: «I like Nutella; Ich liebe Nutella; J'aime Nutella; Me gusta Nutella…».

Nutella has inspired numerous writers and artists from the 1980s onwards.
Left: a watercolor created by the Ligurian painter Eugenio Comencini (in 1999 for the book *Gnam*, like the line drawing on page 4).

Right: the illustration for a Nutella Party to celebrate the advent of the new millennium.

Cinema

In 1984 the Italian film-director Nanni Moretti started the celebration of Nutella with his film *Bianca*, a work that remained in the collective memory of a whole generation. In the film there is mention of the Sacher Torte with the unforgettable phrase: «Ok, let's go on like this, let's do ourselves in». Then, while telling the love story between the school teacher Michele Apicella (Nanni Moretti) and his colleague Bianca (Laura Morante), after a night spent together, the teacher, who is plagued by manias and obsessions, is seen naked eating huge slices of bread spread with Nutella from an enormous jar. In other words, the jar as the ideal cure for the stress of everyday life. As the mass-media expert Alberto Abruzzese stated: for Moretti, Nutella is «pleasure, nourishment, soft Mediterranean form», while «the Viennese cake is rigid and Mitteleuropean». After that citation, cinema again focused its attention on the jar of desire: in Katja von Garnier's *Abgeshminkté* (Making Up!), *Abbronzatissimi* (1991) with the actor Jerry Calà seducing Alba Parietti with a jar of Nutella, and Leonardo Pieraccioni's *I Laureati*, containing the famous quip «What do we want to do? Spend our whole lives regretting Nutella?».

Theater

Riccardo Cassini, an "alternative" author who now writes scripts for the performances of Fiorello, has contributed to making the Nutella icon time-proof. This cabaret artist, discovered by Maurizio Costanzo, achieved notoriety with a one thousand lire booklet published by Panini Comix in 1993 entitled *Nutella Nutellae*. Containing parodies in sham Latin, which he has recited both on stage and on television, it sold more than 300 thousand copies. There have been other artistic performances on stage: in 1991, with *Nutella Amara* by the Società per Attori at the Teatro della Cometa in Rome, written and interpreted by Corrado Guzzanti, and in 1993 with *Una voce quasi umana* (An almost human voice), produced by the Fondazione Sipario Toscana and interpreted by Sonia Grassi.

Music

In a period of over forty years many musical pieces have been dedicated to the "jar", and many Italian songwriters like Gianni Morandi, Gianluca Grignani and Giorgia have confessed their passion for Nutella. In the 1990s there was even a rock group belonging to the Florence rock

Left: the celebration of the thirty-year anniversary of Nutella in France in 1995 with the exhibition «Nutella Génération» held at the Carrousel du Louvre.

Right: the Turin artist Silvano Costanzo next to his creation *Nutpop 2004*, celebrating Nutella's 40th anniversary in Italy in 2004.

underground called *Susy likes Nutella* whose pieces can still be found on YouTube. There is now no trace of the experimental English group *Anesthesia*, who in 1997 included a piece entitled *Nutella Toasted* on their album P.V.C on the Blue Room label. Still receiving many hits on the net is a real treat by Ivan Graziani, with the participation of Renato Zero, from 1995: the song is called *La Nutella di tua sorella* (Your sister's Nutella!). Ironic and amusing, it invites you to use the spread as an alternative to drugs. In the same year another Italian songwriter, the unforgettable Giorgio Gaber, used it as a comparison in his song *Destra-Sinistra* (Right-Left): «I'd say that *culatello* ham is politically to the right and *mortadella* is left. If Swiss chocolate is right, then Nutella is left».

The most recent musical tribute was in 2004 by the television presenter Francesco Facchinetti, who conducted X-Factor and during the Sanremo Festival presented the song *Era bellissimo*. The lyrics include the phrase «my jar full of Nutella» to describe a beloved girlfriend. A few years later the connection between love and the jar came back into fashion in two more songs by young artists. The thirty-year-old Milanese singer Niccolò Cavalchini dedicated to it his 2008 single entitled *Vorrei mangiare la Nutella* (I'd like to eat Nutella) in which he tells how he'd like to share a jar with his girlfriend and «eat only that» all day. A song that for several weeks was one of the ten most downloaded from iTunes in Italy and was also extremely popular in South America.

Various episodes confirming that the Ferrero cream is still a sort of juvenile madeleine of the 21st century, an omnipresent companion through good times and bad. In 2008 the young, neo-melodic Neapolitan singer, Rosario Miraggio, came out with an album of songs that made him known outside of his home area: *Prendere o lasciare* (Take it or leave it). One of the favorite pieces is *Cchiù doce da' Nutella* (Sweeter than Nutella), a love serenade for a beautiful girl. Finally, there is the chamber opera entitled *Nutellam cantata*, written by Maestro Antonello Lerda from Cuneo and inspired by Riccardo Cassini's book. It won second prize at the 'Concorso nazionale di com-

posizione' at La Spezia in 2001 and was represented with a 15-member orchestra, a mezzosoprano, a soprano and a baritone. A joyous and inimitable hymn halfway between Kurt Weill and Stravinsky.

Art The first person to understand that an industrial product could inspire a work of art was Andy Warhol in 1962 when he exhibited his famous *Big Campbell's Soup Can, C. 19 cents*. That technique of solarized color reproduction was used again in 2003 by Ferrero France for a food education campaign.

In 1991 a group of Italian artists influenced by Pop Art created the 'Mistiche Nutelle' group: they had their first exhibition at the Palazzo dei Diamanti in Ferrara, and then others in Bologna, again in 2008 with «Sì logo». Oscar Baccilieri, Vittorio Brocadello, Mauro Luccarini, Maurizio Mantovi and Adriano Tetti wanted to represent «the mystic in art, that combines with the need to go back to being children».

The semiologist Omar Calabrese and the critic Achille Bonito Oliva were intrigued by them. The official artistic consecration was at the Carrousel du Louvre in Paris, from 16 June 1996, with the exhibition *Génération Nutella*: in the show were all the salient works of art that from 1996 had influenced the thirty-year-olds of that time. Many important French artists took part in the exhibition, among them Philippe Découflé, Frank Margerin, Toni Vighetto and the Compagnie Guitoune, which presented the ironic *Machine à Tartiner*.

Other Italian painters have elected Nutella as their muse. Amongst these is the Ligurian artist Eugenio Comencini, who in 1999 created a graphic multiplication of the Nutella jar. *Roxy in the Box* (the Neapolitan Rosaria Bosso) presented her provocative *Femmenella* at the Artissima 2003. And lastly, in *Nutpop 2004* the Piedmontese artist Silvano Costanzo, as part of his research into communication codes, analyzed the passage from a visual language to an occult language: two acrylics on canvas characterized by color tones of a dark purple.

Literature

The symbol of a generation, a vehicle for social values, an image used to convey other ideas, Nutella has been used by writers to describe a sensation, a memory, an atmosphere. In these pages a small anthology of the most significant citations.

Riccardo Cassini: *Nutella Nutellae* (1993). The first book that really turned Nutella into a legend, using the parody of sham Latin.

> *Nutella omnia divisa est in partes tres. Unum: Nutella in vaschetta plasticae. Duum: Nutella in vitreis bicchieribus custodita. Treum: Nutella sita in magno barattolo (magno barattolo sì, sed melium est si magno Nutella in barattolo).*

> All Nutella is divided into three parts. One, Nutella in a plastic tub. Two: Nutella safely kept in a glass jar. Three: Nutella placed in a large jar (a large jar yes, but it's better I eat Nutella from the jar).

Il piccolo libro della Nutella (2000). (The little Nutella book). With many plays on words, the author amuses himself by representing the object of his desire in parodies of well-known songs or Dante's verses, as in the *Divina Nutella*:

> *Midway through this way of life we're bound upon,*
> *I woke to find myself in a dark cream,*
> *Where the right bread roll was completely filled and gone.*

Giuseppe Culicchia: *Tutti giù per terra* (1994). (We all fall down). From the autobiography of Walter, a young unemployed man who drags himself listlessly between the university and the social services center.

> *I would have worked until I was old and on the day I received my pension I would realize I had cancer. I was truly depressed. So I played* **Problems** *by the Sex Pistols and went to the kitchen to hunt for some Nutella.*

Brucia la città (2009). (The city burns). The heroes of a Turin so improbable as to be almost real, in nights without morals or ideals recounted with a frenzied rhythm.

> *[...] and a jar of Nutella and an empty blister of contraceptive pills and a fuchsia pink I-pod nano and a tube of Smarties and new shoes of every color and shape and type, Prada, Miu Miu, Manolo Blahnik, Converse, Nike, Blundstone, Camper. In a corner there was a pink lace 'La Perla' G-string, and well... it looked like an apartment that had been turned over by an investigation squad.*

Gianni Farinetti: *L'isola che brucia* (1997) (The burning island). An ironic portrait of two women in a crime story set against the backdrop of Stromboli, an island the author loves, and the Langhe area of Piedmont.

> *Maria Grazia, ladylike, takes a banana of interesting proportions from the tray. She holds it up to a non-existent audience «...but we don't mind at all...». Ornella is now laughing heartily, her mouth full of Nutella.*

Jacopo Fo: *Ti amo, ma il tuo braccio destro mi fa schifo, tagliatelo* (1998). (I love you, but your right arm disgusts me, cut it off). The son of the Nobel Prize winner for Literature writes of an early erotic encounter.

> *I really liked the idea of «I eat you and you eat me», so one day taking advantage of her parents' week-end absence I take a jar of Nutella and spread it all over myself. Then I hand her the jar ... and her parents walk in!!! I had to throw on my clothes over the Nutella, which is actually difficult technically because it isn't slippery and everything sticks. In short, a rather complicated affair.*

Andrea Lee: *Guilt, Politics, and Eros in a Jar* (1995). The well-known American writer, who has lived in Italy for years, published an article for «The New Yorker» with the aim of making Nutella known to her compatriots.

> *To take the crude step of defining Nutella – pronounced "noo-tella" – as a gooey hazelnut-and-cocoa spread that comes in a jar is a bit like describing the David of Michelangelo as a large carved piece of marble. Like any inspired creation, Nutella has an animating spirit that takes it beyond its physical components.*

Justine Lévy: *The Rendezvous* (1995). The debut novel by the daughter of illustrious Parisian philosopher Bernard-Henri Lévy. The monologue describes an attempted (but unsuccessful) suicide.

> *Disappointed or maybe relieved – what if they'd only been vitamins? I started*
> *wandering through the house, made myself a Nutella sandwich, put on some music,*
> *and rifled through the jewelry box. I tried on some lipstick, some face powder, I put*
> *on fake lashes, but only on one eye, it seemed more chic. After a while, when I felt a*
> *strange tiredness numbing the tips of my fingers, then my legs, I went to lie down on*
> *my mother's bed.*

Margaret Mazzantini: *Venuto al mondo* (2008). (Born into this world). In this novel about a forgotten war, that of Yugoslavia, the writer tells of Gemma's journey to Sarajevo during the siege of 1992. This is the dialogue with her son Pietro, when she tries to persuade him to leave with her.

> *«I have to speak to you».*
> *He rises from the bed, his chest naked.*
> *«I'm so hungry».*
> *«I have to speak to you». He rises from the bed, his chest naked.*
> *So I speak to him in the kitchen as he spreads Nutella on biscuits.*
> *He prepares small sandwiches which he swallows with a single bite.*
> *His mouth is smudged with chocolate, he's covered the table with crumbs, he's opened*
> *the biscuit packet roughly, ripping it all.*
> *I don't say anything, I can't just tell him off all the time.*
> *I look on in silence while he feasts, then I tell him about the trip.*
> *«I don't even want to hear about it, but, you're going on your own...»,*
> *«Look, Sarajevo's a beautiful city...».*

Sebastiano Mondadori: *Un anno fa domani* (2009). (A year ago tomorrow). The protagonist of the novel, Vittorio, manages to win over Teresa, the woman who will become his wife, from her lover, the university professor with whom he's just finished an exam. The two students make love together one night in the professor's house, but he comes home early and finds them in bed. The professor realizes that his relationship with Teresa is over. He then gives Vittorio a few suggestions, while the boy is naked in his bedroom, on how to have a long-lasting sentimental relationship with her.

> *«At any other time I'd probably find you likeable. Since my son would be about your age now, I'm going to give you some advice. Always keep a jar of Nutella and at least two hazelnut chocolate bars at home, better if the chocolate is Novi but Lindt will do».*

Margherita Oggero: *L'amica americana* (2005). (The American friend). Professor Baudino, the female protagonist of a popular series of crime novels by this Turin writer, has a friend among the homeless called Indestructible, who loves one breakfast more than any other.

> *«Indestructible!», she shouted after him, «How about a cappuccino at a coffee shop?» He turned round, squinted, recognized her and stopped. There had been no car accident and no one was running after him. «Cappuccino and croissant with Nutella. You pay».*

Fabio Volo: *Esco a fare due passi* (2001). (I'm just going out for a walk). The real name of this writer, TV presenter and actor is Fabio Bonetti, though he's well known by his stage name. Familiar with the feelings of today's young people, in this novel he tells of a radio disc jockey suffering from Peter Pan syndrome.

> *She had sneaked into that part of the heart where all the good things are, the part that's like a kitchen cupboard filled with cakes and Nutella, biscuits, sweet snacks and jam; that tiny corner of the heart where, when you enter, no matter what, you can't ever leave again. It's got nothing to do with love. There are just some people that when you get to know them you just can't help feeling love for them.*

The web is full of creative elaborations of the legendary spread: above left, the *Nutellisa* created by a Turkish blogger on his website *Café Fernando* and, below, Nutella Day, as envisaged by Sara Rosso and Michelle Fabio.

Above and opposite, top: the homepages of the official websites for Nutella fans: first MyNutella, then Nutellaville, and a page from the institutional website dedicated to *Good Morning Philosophy*. Below, the institutional websites for China, Australia and the United States.

Internut
There is a French group on Facebook called *Le Début du pot de Nutella*, the opening of the Nutella jar. Its hundreds of thousands of members all love that magic moment when the «blade of the knife (not the spoon!) plunges into the still intact cream». This group is of course just one of the many in the Internet celebrating the much-loved hazelnut spread.

But you also find official web pages, like the one started by Ferrero Italy in April 2010, which in just a few months on the most popular social network in Italy has already been visited by more than 1 million 5 hundred thousand people. When asked to recall their first taste of Nutella, visitors' answers bordered on mystical ecstasy. Marianna: «We all grew up on bread and Nutella, and if you're nervous, sad or under stress, bread and Nutella is the winning card, the secret weapon. I still eat it with my grandchildren». Ilenia: «The first time was at my grandmother's house, I was four». Francesca: «How can you remember where or when the first time was? Nutella has always been there... it's part of us». Filippo: «I remember... it was sold by weight... out of big tin boxes and was placed on a piece of grease-proof paper: an unforgettable taste, the amazing 1960s...». Umberto: «Every time I plunge my spoon into Nutella it's just like the first time. Only the spoon has changed, it's gotten bigger!». Lory: «I was really, really little, I know that my mother hid it; I used to climb all over the kitchen to find it... and I always did!».

This is the declared mission: «Welcome to Nutella's official Italian fan page. This page is dedicated to a good breakfast. If "starting off on the right foot" with Nutella is your motto, then stay with us, you won't regret it». This sanctioned the beginning of a change of company strategy towards the new media. After starting the website www.nutella.it (in 2001 in Italy, and subsequently in other countries), in 2003 it started the MyNutella community (www.mynutella.it) where you had to enrol to have your own mini-blog and chat with other Nutella

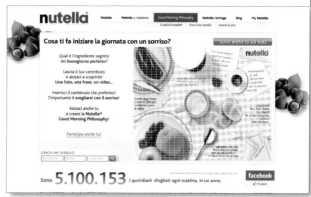

lovers. This space on the Internet was followed in 2008 by Nutellaville (www.nutellaville.it), rather in the style of *Second Life*. But the web runs fast and the prevailing trend now is for social networks. If you type in Nutella on Twitter, you get a message on the subject every few seconds, from the millions of mostly English-speaking users who "twitter" all day. And in the blogs you find all manner of household recipes and interesting tips.

The Web loves Nutella: it's one of the most popular brands in the world. On Facebook, for example, you find at least four pages on Nutella with hundreds of thousands of followers for each; three of these have sprung up spontaneously. And in the names of the pages, infinite variations on the theme: Nutella with crêpes, with croissants, with sandwich bread, spread on a pancake, rolled in a sponge; there is even a request for «the ratification and approval of Nutella as a medicine recognized by the French medical service»; a total of more than 3000 pages.

The classification given by the social network founded by Mark Zuckerberg shows that Nutella has a very good ranking, being among the top ten labels in the world, together with the Starbucks coffee chain, Skittles (sweets), Coca-Cola and Red Bull. Moreover, the jar with the rounded shape receives millions of hits by web users every day on the dozens of official company websites, or on those born out of a love for the product.

Communities of fervent Nutella lovers grow and multiply. At times the material they put on-line is not exactly politically correct, yet they do contribute to the creation of a sort of positive brand equity. In 2004 a statistic on Google gave 176 million search results. Six years later there are six million sites! And Ferrero, judged by a poll in 24 countries, has an excellent corporate reputation: it is ranked first in Italy (June 2010, drawn up by Reputation Institute, with Doxa); at an international level, it is one of only two Italian companies (the other being Barilla) in the top 28 in the world.

Nutella passion | Some like it Spread

Left: the first official Nu-day was held in Piazza San Carlo in Turin on 21 June 2008, with breakfast, snacks, brunch and music concerts in the evening. Far left: the famous Mole Antonelliana was also involved as a symbol of the city.

Facing page: a montage of photo frames for a magical TV advertisement that was very successful in the 2003 Christmas period.

As the language of marketing explains, Nutella is an «inclusive» brand, which means that everyone feels a little bit part of it, whereas for other cult brands the exact opposite can happen: «exclusive tribes» are formed around a perfume or a motorcycle that others cannot get to.

Healthy, visionary, rational, emotional, in the last ten years an "Internut" network has been consolidated. That's how we should re-name this Web that lures spontaneous groups of people or organizes promotions. On 5 February 2007, two American girls who live in Italy and are passionate food-writers and photographers – Sara Rosso and Michelle Fabio – launched their very first World Nutella Day, which every year attracts thousands of enrollees. On the occasion, a well-known Turkish food blogger, through his website *Café Fernando*, launched an image that became immediately popular, the figure of a woman reminiscent of a portrait by the famous artist Botero: he called her Nutellisa. It was a global success. Cenk Sonmezsoy (who writes on cookery from Istanbul after having studied in San Francisco), Sara and Michelle have no involvement with the Ferrero company in any way: what they do, they do for love, they do out of their passion for Nutella.

The only outing ever arranged by Nutellaville was a day-long party in Turin on 21 June 2008, in Piazza San Carlo and in the Parco del Valentino: breakfast, brunch and afternoon snacks with songs and music courtesy of the Aram Quartet (of X-Factor fame), Meg and Max Gazzé. A day given over to «good humor, relaxation and positive thinking» with the main garden in Turin transformed into a sort of *déjeuner sur l'herbe*. And to think that it had all started in the year 2000 with Gnutella, a protocol made to share musical files by two California boys, with a name inspired by the famous spread and by "Gnu", the free software system made operative by Unix.

A rapid "spreading of the word" on the web followed that was undoubtedly helped by the catchy name, thanks to which it even defeated the giant Napster. Justin Frankel and Tom Pepper then realized they couldn't go against Ferrero by imitating their trademark and thus they avoided heavy legal battles. This "peer-to-peer" system is now obsolete, but it used to be the first way to spread songs in Mp3 over the world's computers. Free.

Nutella passion | Some like it Spread

Periodo promozionale 20/11/2003 - 29/02/2004. Valore montepremi 300.000,00 €

Regolamento completo su www.nutella.it e sulle cartoline promozionali

Che mondo sarebbe senza Nutella

Regolamento completo su www.nutella.it e sulle cartoline promozionali

Left: the manufacturing plant of Ferrero in Somerset, New Jersey, United States, where Nutella was produced for a few years.

Facing page: one of the advertisements of the publicity campaign launched in 2010 all over the United States, and the article which appeared on the front page of the «Herald Tribune» in December 2004.

A star and stripes cream   Sabrina, Tyler, Arianna, Ashley, George, Jesse, Massimiliano, Tiziano... these are some of the names of children aged from 7 to 17 printed on the «Golden Microphone» diploma given to me on 23 October 2006 by the Italian Culture Institute of New York, on Broadway. On this occasion I met the children who were pupils attending the Italian courses of the *Italian American Committee on Education*, as part of the «journalist for a day» project. A few days later, the daily New York paper «America Today» published a review of the conference in which a writer had actually dedicated a book to Nutella, to the great surprise of the young American public. If Sabrina confessed that at home she ate Nutella on unleavened bread because she was Jewish, others showed brightly colored drawings in which the identity card of the product was described: zodiac sign, Aries, since it was born on the 20th of April; parents: «father Giandujot» and «mother Supercrema»; distinguishing features: «the most famous snack in the world».

Two years earlier the «Herald Tribune», the American daily newspaper published in Paris, calling me the «most famous Italian Nutellologist», had in fact covered the cultural and political aspects of the product. On the front page it wrote that it made no sense to assert that «Nutella is left and Swiss chocolate is right». In fact, to underline this bi-partisan point of view, Cinzia Scaffidi of Slow Food sustains that it is in fact a «glocal» product. It is also inter-classist, because, like pasta, it is eaten and enjoyed by every social group, «from peasants to princes». Nobody has ever contested Nutella in protests against globalization or against the enormous power of the multinational companies. «Every generation», continued the newspaper, quoting the opinion of the expert

nutella
The original hazelnut spread®

At breakfast, you can use all the help you can get. That's why there's Nutella.®

A unique hazelnut spread made from wholesome ingredients such as roasted hazelnuts, skim milk and a hint of delicious cocoa. Use Nutella® spread on all kinds of nutritious foods — like multigrain toast — to add a touch of flavor and give your kids a tasty breakfast you can feel good about.

- More than 50 hazelnuts per 13 oz. jar
- No artificial colors or preservatives
- Made with high-quality ingredients

Nutella®...Breakfast never tasted this good!
www.NutellaUSA.com

© FERRERO

Visit www.NutellaUSA.com to learn how Nutella® can add great taste to your balanced breakfast.

INTERNATIONAL
Herald Tribune

THE WORLD'S DAILY NEWSPAPER PUBLISHED BY **THE NEW YORK TIMES** EDITED IN PARIS AND PRINTED IN BOLOGNA
FRIDAY, DECEMBER 10, 2004

The politics of Nutella

Italy is abuzz as hazelnut spread turns 40

By Elisabetta Povoledo

BRA, Italy: Is Nutella, the chocolate hazelnut spread, left- or right-wing?

"Only Italians could turn something like this into an ideological question," said Gigi Padovani, who put the question to a group of students at the Velso Mucci Institute, a technical school for chefs and waiters in this small town in northern Italy.

As the dark creamy treat turns 40, intellectuals throughout the country have been debating what Padovani calls the "cultural, social, artistic and gastronomic phenomenon" that is Nutella.

"It's only here that people say that a shower is 'left' while a bath is 'right,' jeans are 'left,' a jacket is 'right,' or that Nutella is 'left' and Swiss Chocolate is 'right,'" said Padovani, setting off titters among the students.

He was teasing, but he had a point to make: "All generations have appropriated Nutella — they all feel as though it belongs to them. It transcends generations. It is national-popular," he said, referring to a concept coined by the founder of the Italian Communist Party, Antonio Gramsci. "Today we would call it bipartisan."

Padovani, who writes for the Turin daily La Stampa, is the author of "Nutella, un mito italiano," (Nutella, an Italian myth).

As Italy's foremost "Nutellologist," he has had a busy year, traveling around the country, and Europe, lecturing on the pervasive popularity of his gooey specialty.

Eulogized in print, in song, and on screen, Nutella is one of those rare products that have transcended their nature as food to enter the collective consciousness.

NUTELLA, Continued on Page 6

Sandro Castaldo, «has made Nutella its own, thanks partly to superb advertising which only 10 years after the product's first appearance credited it with being the favorite food of mothers of the previous generation». The conclusion was: Nutella is nationally popular, better still, it represents an independent ideology, that of *buonismo*, «the Italian tendency to envelop everything in something sweet, something that serves to conceal any difficulty and make life pleasing». «This», concluded the newspaper, on the first page of the 10th of December 2004, «is the essence of being Italian: goodness that you can spread».

Americans, thank partly to the articles of Andrea Lee, have had many opportunities to get to know Nutella. It must be mentioned, however, that in the context of the extraordinary success of Italian food all over the world Nutella didn't become as famous there as Parmigiano Reggiano or prosciutto. The French consider it as being French, the Germans are convinced it is «made in Germany», the Belgians believe it originated in Flanders or was created by the Walloons. It has been around in the United States for twenty years, although more as a specialty product: American consumers tend not to consider it as the Europeans do. Well known in university campuses and appreciated by gourmets, our hazelnut cream has been "dueling" with peanut butter since 1985. For a long time it was just a little luxury imported from Europe.

But lately things have been changing. Because a small production of Nutella began in Somerset, New Jersey, not far from Newark airport, where you can still find Ferrero's US headquarters. Then in October 2006 factory production was moved to Ontario in Canada, to Brantford, a city of almost one hundred thousand inhabitants

Nutella passion | Some like it Spread

THE NEW YORKER

THE TALK OF THE TOWN

FROM ITALY: GUILT, POLITICS, AND EROS IN A JAR

It's time Americans took a good, hard look at Nutella. Not many of us are familiar with this singular Italian food product, which could be the means of liberating ourselves from an inferiority complex that has dogged us for at least the last twenty years—complex based on the tormenting belief that all Italian food is healthier and more natural than the corrupt, mass-produced American alternative. We tend to envision Italians at meals as being gathered in pastoral family groups around vast alfresco tables in the shade of millennial olive trees, scarfing down handmade pasta, sun-dried tomatoes, ripe figs, buffalo mozzarella, and other salubrious dainties that suggest centuries-old peasant ties to the fecund Mediterranean soil. Instead, the average Italian is just as likely to be found indoors in front of a Berlusconi-televised tap-dancing girlie spectacular, devouring Nutella, one of the world's great junk foods and a substance just as fresh from the factory as a brand-new Fiat.

To take the crude step of defining Nutella—pronounced "noo-tell"—as a gooey hazelnut-and-chocolate spread that comes in a jar is a bit like describing the David of Michelangelo as a large curved piece of marble. Like any inspired creation, Nutella has an animating spirit that takes it beyond its physical components. Shamelessly sweet but not too sweet, more unctuous than peanut butter but with the same curiously sexy capacity for gluing the jaws together, and intensely chocolate-flavored but with a peculiar pillowy mildness that appeals to regressive urges, it is made to be spread on bread but more often ends up being eaten in hasty spoonfuls straight from the jar. It costs little, and tastes better than most of the decadent desserts that posh restaurants baptize with names like Quadruple Chocolate Ganache in a Coulis of Fresh Madagascar Cacao Bean Purée. Though Nutella is marketed as a snack for children, everyone knows that it's packed with more sugar and fat per ounce than Oprah Winfrey on an ice-cream binge. It's naughty

and it's addictive, as its popularity inside and outside Italy attests. Millions of jars of Nutella are sold in Europe, Japan, and parts of South America every year; it has become chic in Paris sidewalk cafés and is even rumored to have been glimpsed in Kenya.

To Italians, Nutella has become a cult. Developed after the Second World War as an industrial version of a traditional homemade chocolate-hazelnut delicacy called gianduja, the spread appealed to the hunger for cheap sweets in the lean postwar years, when bread and chocolate was a treat that children dreamed of. The increasing national love for Nutella kept pace with Italy's four-decade journey from poverty to world industrial power. Everybody under fifty seems to have childhood Nutella memories of blissful after-school snacks, of midnight raids on the kitchen nooks where Mamma hid the jar. Everybody's ex-spouse seems to have become Nutella-dependent during the low point of the marriage. Recently, innumerable famous personages, among them the singer Gianni Morandi, have publicly confessed their addiction. In 1990, a journalist in La Stampa wrote of Nutella, "A devouring passion. Uncontrollable. It has struck heads of state, bewitched artists, reduced poets. The love for Nutella is inexplicable, it just is. ... More than a food, it is a category of the spirit, a state of superior perception." When, in the same year, a young satiric publisher published a comic pamphlet eulogizing Nutella in Spanish, English, French, and Latin (excerpt: "Nutella omnia divisa est in partes tres"), the work sold a hundred and fifty thousand copies in three months.

Like any squishy chocolate food with infantile associations, Nutella is obliquely linked not only to guilt but to Eros. The erotic factor came fully out of the closet this past Christmas, when the New Open Gate, the most fashionable club in Rome, put on an Il Primo Nutella Party, featuring hundreds of jars and an eight-metre baguette slathered with the stuff. In the course of what was described as an extraordinarily success-

ful evening, guests spread it on their partners and licked it off.

The Nutella party was sponsored by a local branch of Forza Italia, the political organization of then Prime Minister Silvio Berlusconi. Only a few days later, Berlusconi resigned. Coincidence? Pundits will no doubt argue for years over the extent of the occult role of a chocolate spread in the tempestuous fortunes of fin-de-siècle Italian governments, but one thing is certain: ever in tune with the Italian soul, Nutella in the nineties has become publicly associated with the newly powerful right-wing establishment. In an article discussing the political implications of the Nutella party—entitled "WHAT COLOR IS NUTELLA?"—the weekly news magazine Panorama quoted Teodoro Buontempo, a notorious hard-liner of the ultraconservative National Alliance: "Nutella is definitely right wing. With its solidity, it gives an idea of well-being; yet it is also fluid, and it strikes the imagination."

However, in the same article a centrist-minded spokesman for Forza Italia declared soothingly that its mixing images of traditional family values with the low-priced mass consumption valued by the left, Nutella represents a future ideologically united Italy—presumably an Italy in which the lion lies down with the lamb and everyone licks his neighbor.

What should the United States' position on Nutella be? The first appropriate response for sensible Americans is a sigh of relief and an abandonment of all those complexes we have about the Mediterranean diet. The second should be to demand from our leaders immediate Nutella importation and distribution. Some jars have been sighted in supermarkets across the country, but not nearly enough for these unsettled times. There is no reason that New World citizens should not look to the Old World for solutions. After all, it was a proto-Italian commentator who came up with one of the earliest and best suggestions for keeping a nation happy. Instead of bread and circuses, we can easily make do with bread and chocolate.

Left: the article written by Andrea Lee, published by the prestigious «The New Yorker» in 1995, did much to familiarize the American public with Nutella.

A supermarket display of Nutella jars in the United States: the hazelnut spread has been sold all over the country since 2008.

Facing page: an artistic interpretation of the legendary jar in Andy Warhol style, from a Ferrero France advertisement of 2003.

founded by Joseph Brant, a native American Indian. The Ferrero group has made a considerable investment in the area, an unprecedented move considering the tentative steps taken in the past when developing outside of Italy: this means that Ferrero is determined to take Nutella, Tic Tac and Rocher into the NAFTA markets (Canada, USA and Mexico).

The initial word of mouth publicity started with young American soldiers stationed in Europe, who enjoyed Nutella for breakfast and when back in the States proceeded to spread it throughout their home towns. Then in 2010 a massive publicity campaign was launched, with advertisements in magazines and on television to let housewives know that it's not just a topping for a cup cake or to use as a decoration but an everyday «quick and easy» food to give children as they start their day, delicious on America's wonderful white bread.

During our American tour, with my wife Clara, the chefs who took part in creating this book enthusiastically agreed to "invent" some recipes with Nutella. Some of them already had dishes with the hazelnut spread on their menus. And one of them even replied: «Nutella? Of course, my child finishes off a jar in one week... ».

Nutella passion | Some like it Spread

LETTERS IN A JAR

DICTIONARY OF NAMES AND CURIOSITIES

by Gigi Padovani

A

ALBA

Dawn, the hour before the rising of the sun, but also the name of an old city in southern Piedmont, 40 miles from Turin, famous for its white truffles and for having been the birth-place of Nutella. Over its medieval towers wafts the intoxicating scent of toasted hazelnuts and cocoa. In the old town center (**below, a view of the cathedral**) you can still see the small courtyard where Pietro Ferrero opened his first shop in 1945. In December 2009 the Italian weekly magazine «Panorama» published a list which classified the quality of life in Italian cities, a sort of "overall well-being" list drawn up by the Centro Studi Sintesi of Venice. Alba won second place in the ranking, after the town of Brunico. Could it be the air of Nutella making everyone happy?

ALLEVI

Giovanni: the most famous young classical music composer in Italy, indulges in a special breakfast when he's on tour. As he explained to Giancarlo Dotto: «I gave myself Nutella as a prize» («La Stampa», 27 July 2009).

B

BANYULS

A naturally sweet French wine from the Roussillon area, very near the border with Spain, which enhances the aromatic notes of chocolate. For Enzo Vizzari, a well-known gourmet and director of the «Espresso» Food Guide, it combines excellently with Nutella: «Nutella is good. In fact, for adult consumers I would recommend eating it together with a glass of Banyuls» («Messaggero», 18 April 2004).

BERLUSCONI

Silvio: businessman, politician, prime minister, one of the richest and best known Italians in the world. His son, Pier Silvio, born in 1969 from his first marriage with Carla dell'Oglio, in an interview with «Men's Health» in November 2006, declared that he kept in shape with constant physical exercise and two or three times a week indulged in some Nutella.

BELLUCCI/BINOCHE

Juliette Binoche, the French actress who won international acclaim with the film *Chocolat*, has often admitted to eating «spoonfuls of Nutella». The beautiful Italian actress Monica Bellucci has also said: «I love eating, the greatest pleasure of all is a salami sandwich immediately followed by one with Nutella» («La Repubblica», 5 July 1994).

BLOB

Originally an American movie (*The Blob*, 1958) with slimy monsters, in Italy it is known as a sequence of video excerpts mounted in rapid succession. The technique has been used mercilessly in the TV programme created by Enrico Ghezzi and Marco Giusti, who from 1989 have "punished" numerous TV personalities. It is also a term coined by the semiologist Omar Calabrese, who describes Nutella as «a good blob».

BOCUSE

Paul: the French chef and inventor of *nouvelle cuisine* told the journalist Fiammetta Fadda of his sinful predilection: «A madeleine straight from the oven spread with Nutella» («Panorama», March 2007).

CAROSELLO (Merry-go-round)

On 3 February 1957, the debut on RaiUno of this cult transmission – the first vehicle for TV advertisements. For over twenty years (until 1 January 1977) the protagonists of those sketches accompanied the evenings of the Italian people, and after it, traditionally, children went happily to bed. Nutella first appeared on *Carosello* in 1966, with the cartoons called *Le Memorie di un diplomatico* (*Memoirs of a Diplomat*) by the Pagot brothers.

COLAZIONE (Breakfast)

In an English breakfast, you expect tea, toast, butter, jam and fried eggs. But since Nutella became a citizen of Europe, it has become part of the breakfast ritual for millions of people. To commemorate the 40-year anniversary of the product in

Germany, in a large sports arena a breakfast was prepared worthy of the Guinness Book of Records: on 29 May 2005, in the Aufschalke Arena in Gelsenkirchen (40 miles from Dortmund), 27,854 people shared a Nutella breakfast, beating the previous "most people at breakfast" record in Thailand.

COROLLA

Do you like dipping fresh fruit in Nutella? Then why not create a round plastic tray to make it easier. This idea inspired Isaac Pinero and Alessandro Stabile: in December 2008, with the Corolla project, they won the competition promoted by the design magazine «Interni». The two young designers produced their prototype (**photo, below**) at the Polytechnic School of Design in Milan. Isaac now works in Valencia, Spain, with the Nadadora Studio. Seventy project designers

D

participated from 10 schools of design or universities, from Milan, Turin, Venice, Rome, Naples and Palermo.

CORYLUS AVELLANA

This is the scientific name for the hazelnut. Toasted and mixed with cocoa it gives us the best products in Italian confectionery. Its greatest merit is having inspired the name Nutella. The hazelnut is in fact an important health food. It is recommended for anyone with cholesterol problems because it naturally lowers high levels due to its content of oleic acid. It also contains monounsaturated fats, that is "friendly" fats, and contains a higher quantity of vitamin E than any other type of dried fruit.

CRÊPES

These little pancakes, made with eggs, flour and milk, whether savory or sweet, are one of the most popular French national dishes. On the 2nd of February each year, France celebrates *Chandeleur*, an old religious tradition dedicated to light, in which candles are blessed and you say good-bye to winter. By tradition, you should eat *crêpes*, especially with Nutella – in fact this is the day of the greatest consumption of the Ferrero cream. The custom is spreading quickly in Italy too, so much so that in 2005 one of the oldest manufacturers of household goods, Ballarini (established in 1889), launched a new product called *iLoveCookingCrêpes* (**above**) which inside the carton has a special crêpe griddle, the *crêpière*, a crêpe batter spreader, a spatula, and a jar of Nutella.

CUCCIARI

Geppi: this humorous Sardinian actress has conquered the Italian theatre-going public with her comedy show *Si vive una volta. Sola* (a play on words, she turns the phrase "You only live once" to "You live once. Alone!"). Her tour started in 2007 and has been so popular that it's been going ever since. Miss Cucciari carries her sturdy rounded figure with perfect ease both on stage and on television, and in her play describes the world of a stressed-out woman with «many jars of Nutella and few dates with men».

DESIGN

It's not only good, it's beautiful. Thanks to its sinuous jar which continues to reap success. In fact, in April 2006, at the Furniture Show in Milan, the designers Michelangelo Giombini, Matteo Migliorini and Marco Sarno presented three projects for "NutMobili" inspired by the shape of the jar: a streamline 1950s fridge, a contemporary chest of drawers in polycarbonate and zebra effect wood and an antique late 19th-century chest of drawers (**photo, below**).

DEVOTO-OLI

In 1960 Giacomo Devoto, a linguist of the Accademia della Crusca and Gian Carlo Oli, professor in Italian institutes of culture abroad, published the first edition of their Italian lan-

E

guage dictionary, which is one of the most widely used. In the 1995 edition a new word appeared: «nutella s.f. (*nu-tél-la*) the trade name of a popular hazelnut and cocoa spread». The Ferrero company, fearing that the brand name might become "popularized", obtained from the authors, in following editions, the written specification that Nutella was a "registered trademark", as required by European Community legislation.

DUCASSE

Alain: not only a great chef, but now a successful manager, having founded a business group incorporating almost thirty restaurants from all over the world. One day Ducasse confided to us: «Nutella? Yes, it's true. I adore it. When I'm in my New York restaurant I always have a huge 10 lb jar nearby» (from the *Dolcelavita* blog, LaStampa.it, 19 April 2009).

ENERGY

The basis for the first rule of thermodynamics is the equivalence between work and heat. How to explain it nicely? Well, it's been done by the physicist Monica Marelli in her intriguing book *La fisica del tacco 12* (The physics of a 4½" heel). This is what she writes in relation to dietary problems that can arise from abuse of the "jar": «It's the fault of the first law of thermodynamics: the energy of Nutella enjoyed = the energy of Nutella stored and/or consumed».

EROS

What's Nutella got to do with love? Well, erotic dreams associated with transgressive use of the product abound. Eros and Nutella, as far as the search for pleasure goes, can only go together well, to quote Sigmund Freud. Chocolate is, of course, frequently regarded as an aphrodisiac, even though

sexologist Willy Pasini is convinced that any food can be exciting on the basis of the expectations it generates. The andrologist Maurizio Bossi, referring to the ambiguous hermaphroditism of chocolate (in Italian the word "chocolate" is feminine when it's warm and liquid, becoming masculine when cold and solidified), claims that the creaminess of Nutella is more maternal and reassuring as an alternative kind of love. This is underlined by the journalist Maria Latella in an article published at the dawn of the year 2000 on things to keep or throw away from the 1900s. Among the things to keep she mentions Nutella. «A providential instrument for women in crisis and film-directors called Nanni, it risks going down in history for marginal details like its symbolic association with Walter Veltroni. But while politicians come and go, physiological needs remain: for unhappy love affairs Nutella will remain unbeatable».

EVEREST

In the Himalayan mountain range, between Nepal and Tibet, is the highest mountain in the world. Many Italian mountain climbers who have scaled Everest had Nutella jars in their rucksacks. The former Olympic cross-country skiing champion Manuela Di Centa was regrettably robbed of hers. She was in Nepal during the Everest Speed Expedition when someone stole what she declared was her most treasured possession: the jars of Nutella («La Gazzetta dello Sport», 15 April 2003).

EUROCHOCOLATE

The biggest and best-known exhibition on chocolate in Italy, which ever since 1994 has taken place in Perugia in the autumn. The exhibition was the idea of the architect Eugenio Guarducci, and draws hundreds of thousands of passionate lovers of the "food of the gods". During the 1995 edition the first Nutella Party was organized, strictly in pajamas. And in the year 2000, a great Nutelleria was set up in Piazza Castello in Turin (**photo, opposite**).

FINGER BISCUIT

Who has never felt the temptation to dip their finger into a newly opened jar of spreading cream? Now you can do better: an object presented at the Milan Furniture Show in 2006 and then at the *Tra gioco e discarica* exhibition in 2010 at the Triennale Design Museum in Milan. It's the curious *Finger biscuit* (**photo below, some prototypes**), designed by Paolo Ulian: a biscuit you don't hold in your hand but you slip onto your finger like a thimble and eat in one bite, coated with Nutella. An ingenious idea that does away with guilt feelings.

FERRO

Tiziano: awarded a prize as the "best-selling" Italian singer at the World Music Awards, the pop-star, born in Latina, told Marinella Venegoni of his passion for cooking. His speciality? «Sbrisolona alla Nutella» («La Stampa», 29 March 2009).

G

FIORELLO

Rosario: probably the most popular television showman in Italy. Born in Catania in 1960, he learnt to entertain in tourist resorts along the coast and later became successful with a karaoke program on Mediaset, then on RAI (together with a hugely popular radio show) and finally on Sky. Here, during a show on 16 May 2009, he sang the praises of Michele Ferrero, the inventor of Nutella. To a laughing public he said: «I liked Nutella so much when I was a kid that I'd spread it on my wounds; I'd graze my knee, rub Nutella on it, and I'd feel fine. That's where "licking your wounds" comes from». Then he mused: «Why moms, after buying Nutella, did you always hide it?», ending the show with: «Nutella isn't just a cream you eat, it's a whole world…».

G8

Breakfast on the last morning of the G8 summit held in Aquila, at the Coppito barracks, on 10 July 2009, was based on Nutella, fresh fruit and milk: serving it was the chef of the Italian national soccer team, Claudio Silvestri, with his assistant Andrea Giovannini. Both have appeared in Ferrero TV ads for years.

GARKO

The pseudonym of Dario Gabriel Oliviero, born in Turin in 1974. He's an actor greatly loved by the female public, and a leading actor in numerous television series. He has told interviewers of having had a sweet childhood, being the son of a pastry chef: «Even now I adore Nutella» («Anna», December 2007).

GIGANTE AMICO (Friendly Giant)

A humungous man, who is usually scary, but can also be a friend. Romano Bertola is a Turin writer and inventor of comic strips, and the author of many jingles and slogans for the world of advertising that have been greatly loved by the Italian public, like the little Dutch girl used by Mira Lanza, the Maria Rosa of Bertolini, and the Merendero for the products of Talmone. His best-loved invention was Gigante Amico (the Friendly Giant) (**illustration, left**), a character in the cartoon series created by the Pagot brothers that was broadcast on Italian television between 1971 and 1976. Who exactly was the Friendly Giant? In reality it was the Ferrero Company dispensing help and sweets to children.

H

GILLI (or the Cube)

If you love Nutella and you want to show it, and if you're willing to pay over € 500 for a "limited edition" bag made by Gilli (the brand created by Giulia Ligresti), then the "Nutella Cube" is perfect for you. It's made from brown and white calfskin with a nappa finish and represents the legendary jar (**photo, below**): the patent leather applications reproduce the bread slice, the glass of milk, and the hazelnuts of the label. It was given as a gift to the first ladies present at the G8 meeting in Abruzzo in 2009, and is admired by such Italian actresses as Serena Autieri, Milly Carlucci and Nancy Brilli.

HEGEL

The German idealist philosopher Georg W. Friedrich Hegel claimed that the spirit is universal consciousness, rationality that manifests in reality. But then there are those who believe that it can be expressed in the fabled Ferrero cream, like the journalist Laura Carassai, who when reviewing the book by Cassini, *Nutella Nutellae*, wrote: «A devouring passion. Unstoppable. It has been the obsession of heads of state, bewitched artists, seduced poets. The love for Nutella cannot be explained, it just "is". The hazelnut spread with the taste of gianduia is more than just food, it's a category of the spirit, a higher state of perception» («La Stampa», 8 October 1993).

HELVETICA MEDIUM

One of the most traditional and legible print-types. In the 1960s it was used by Studio Stile in Milan, the graphic studio that designed the Nutella logo, which has remained almost unchanged. The letters of the logo were red with only the initial letter in black.

HOWE

Andrew: born in the United States, in Los Angeles, in 1985 and a naturalized Italian. In 2006 he won the European long jump title. What is the perfect diet for Andrew? He has declared: «I eat everything, but with my mind. Obviously you need to be able to satisfy some whim or fancy. I too have my small jar of Nutella» («La Gazzetta dello Sport», 10 April 2008).

Nutella passion | Letters in a Jar

I

IRAQ

Once called Mesopotamia, it is now a state in the middle of international tensions after the war that deposed the dictator Saddam Hussein. Even in Iraq, far from home, a jar of Nutella can bring comfort. In Bassora, on 28 March 2003, when the attack on Saddam had just started, a jeep with seven Italian journalists was stopped in the suburbs, while the British army was about to invade the town. Arrested by local militia, they were held for 12 days by Iraqi soldiers before being freed in Baghdad by the American army. In his diary, one of the reporters, Luciano Galli, wrote of a painful theft: «Where's the jar of Nutella? In the baggage trunk. Bedlam. They're grabbing everything they can lay their hands on. Let's save what we can». But the Nutella jar had already disappeared («Il Giornale», 10 April 2003).

ISOLA (Island)

A portion of land, surrounded by water. But there's a special one, the sweetest in the world. It's surrounded by the largest confectionery manufacturing plant in Europe, covering an area of 400 thousand square meters. It's the building called Isola Nutella, Nutella Island, and it's at Alba, where giant vats are constantly at work making the famous cream.

ITALIA

Nutella has become part of what identifies the concept of "made in Italy". Its «extraordinary combination of taste, spreadability and packaging» – according to the definition of the Catalog for the exhibition *Cento anni di prodotto italiano (1900-2000)* (One hundred years of Italian products), held in 2001 on the initiative of the Parco Scientifico Tecnologico Galileo of Padua – made it, according to a survey among visitors, the favorite of all the exhibits on display: from the Vespa to the Fiat Cinquecento. And at the exhibition *Italianità* (from which a book was published, edited by Giulio Iacchetti), held at the Galleria Corraini in Mantua at the end of 2008, Nutella was of course represented (**illustration, left**) among the thirty objects on show that have contributed to making up the Italian "visual consciousness", together with the trademarks Agip, Apecar, Coppa Del Nonno, the Graziella bicycle, Moka Bialetti, Pastiglie Leone, the trousers worn by Italian Carabinieri… These objects were all represented in a surreal and creative way on large panels painted by Ale+Ale, better known as Alessandro Lecis and Alessandra Panzeri.

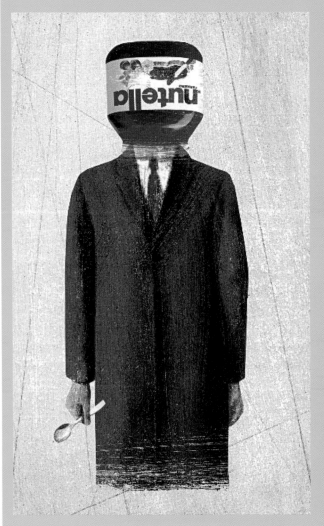

J

L

JO CONDOR

The Spencer Tracy film *A Guy Named Joe* was a huge success in Italy after the war. Romano Bertola, a Turin advertiser, was inspired by it to create the character Jo Condor (**illustration, below**), the enemy of the Friendly Giant. Those who watched *Carosello* will recall the memorable gag of the pilot bird: «E che, c'ho scritto, Jo Condor?» (Hey, have I got Jo Condor written on my forehead?), with the background chorus singing: «Friendly Giant... you take care of it», calling for his help against the persecutors of the tranquil village. The phrase could be traced back to Piedmontese tradition. «*Ho scritto giocondo sulla fronte*?» (Have I got Giocondo written on my forehead?). A way of saying: I'm not stupid.

LAVIER

Bertrand: the French artist born in Châtillon-sur-Seine in 1949 transforms objects of everyday use into works of art. And what could be more worldwide than Nutella? So a pallet of about 800 jars of Nutella was exhibited by Lavier, together with other multimedia installations, at the *Sons & Lumières* exhibition in Reims, in 2009, for the 6th edition of *Expérience Pommery*, a show held every year in the cellars of the great champagne producers.

LIBÉRATION

The most non-conformist French daily newspaper dedicated a page written by Eric Jozsef on Nutella's 40th anniversary. In the article he describes how Nutella has become «un mito», a legend, a sort of «*condensé de l'Italie*», a summary or condensation of Italy, even if one doubt remains: «*Le ou la Nutella, comme disent les Italiens, masculin ou féminin?*» (Le or la Nutella, as the Italians say, is it masculine or feminine?) («Libération», 29 January 2005).

Nutella passion | Letters in a Jar

MADELEINE

A traditional French tea cake (**below**), shaped like a small shell, though the word is known mostly for its Proustian connection which comes from a famous passage of the book *In Search of Lost Time* in which the protagonist, while eating a cake, remembers the madeleines his aunt Léonie used to prepare for him on Sunday mornings. Marcel Proust was recalling the cakes of his own childhood. In 1990 the Italian journalist Rita Cirio published a book in France dedicated to the most famous objects "made in Italy". She included the Nutella jar: «Whole generations grew up with its flavor, which resembles chocolate but isn't, and its soft consistency, sweet and slightly gooey: a kind of Proustian madeleine, spreadable and shared by all».

MARCEGAGLIA

Emma: a steel entrepreneur, and the first woman in Italy to become president of the Italian Confindustria, the organization representing all the industrialists in the country. Elected on 13 March 2008, she told Raffaella Polato about the rituals of summer holidays at the seaside: «We used to go running and swimming. And then we'd get rid of all the fatigue with two spoons and a jar of Nutella» («Corriere della Sera», 13 March 2008).

MAMMA

Possibly the first word any of us say. According to some psychologists, the fabled hazelnut spread is a sort of "big mother" for Italians. And for thirteen years Ferrero used advertising slogans evoking that sentiment, claiming «*Mamma tu lo sai*» (Mommy, you know). In the background the song *Vola colomba* by Nilla Pizzi, the advertisement showed scenes of daily life in the 1950s. And a voice-over saying: «Life was more natural. Your mother took care of everything for you. This is why you grew up well and happy. Do you remember? Your mom used to give you Nutella».

McCONAUGHEY

Matthew: the American actor, born in Texas in 1969, is considered by many the new Paul Newman. He has been involved sentimentally with Sandra Bullock and Penelope Cruz, has a statuary physique, but doesn't give anything up: «Sometimes that spoonful of Nutella that you want so badly, just eat it. You have to give in to temptation every now and again» («Ok benessere prevenzione», November 2009).

N

NAPOLEON

Born in Ajaccio, in Corsica, the army officer who later became emperor to the French, Napoleon Bonaparte is one of the most widely discussed figures in history. He had already been in power for six years when he issued the Berlin Decree (1806), with which he forbade the entry of all British ships and any ships that had stopped over in British ports. Colonial products arrived in Europe along these routes, and from that time on the price of these goods rose steeply. This included cocoa (not yet cultivated in Africa, where it would arrive only in 1822). At this time Turin was the chocolate capital of Italy and its confectioners decided to use hazelnuts, easily found in the Langhe hills, as a substitute for cocoa. In 1865, successfully mixing ground hazelnuts, cocoa and sugar into a deli-

cious mixture, they created *Gianduiotto* chocolate, the ancestor of Nutella. Interestingly enough, in 2005 the Ferrero Foundation paid homage to the French Emperor with an exhibition dedicated to "Napoleon and Piedmont". It was inaugurated by the French actor Gérard Depardieu, who has played Napoleon Bonaparte several times and who agreed to come to Alba on two conditions (as referred by the Ansa press agency, 5 August 2005). The first: a gargantuan lunch based on white Alba truffles. The second: a provision of Nutella equal to his weight. They accepted.

NOBEL

Alfred Bernhard: the Swedish chemist who invented dynamite in 1875. Nobel assigned part of his patrimony for the prizes that each year the Academy of Science in Stockholm awards to benefactors of mankind in various fields: physics, chemistry, medicine, literature and peace. Between 1991 and 1992, the satirical weekly «Cuore» (Heart), directed by Michele Serra, carried out a permanent survey among its readers based on «the five things worth living for». It was called the «Last Judgment» and even today survives as a little encyclopedia of Italian passions. Nutella regularly ranked mid-table. From the pages of «Cuore» Fabio Fazio asked: «Why don't they give the Nobel prize for Literature to the inventor of Nutella?».

NUTELLERIA

A place of delight and gluttony, organized in 1999 and 2000 at the Bologna Motor Show and at the celebrations of the Eurochocolate exhibitions of Perugia and Turin. At a Nutelleria you can taste and enjoy pizzas, piadine, crêpes, mousses, fruit salads and shakes, all, obviously, made with Nutella. In the summer of 2005, a *Table Nutella* was prepared in Paris (**photo, left**) to celebrate the first 40 years of the product in France. The atmosphere was more that of a chic lounge than a fast-food place.

Nutella passion | Letters in a Jar

O

OLIMPIADI INVERNALI (Winter Olympics)

The modern Olympics, that take their name from the games that were held in Olympia in ancient Greece, to honor Zeus, were started in 1896 on the initiative of De Coubertin. The Winter Olympics were first held in Chamonix, in France, in 1924. Arianna Fontana, a young blonde from Valtellina (near Sondrio) became the youngest Italian to win a medal; the bronze in Turin in 2006 when only 15 years old, followed by another third position in Vancouver, Canada, in 2010. Her speciality is the short track. But her passion is: «an inevitable breakfast with Nutella» («La Provincia di Como», 19 February 2010).

ORWELL

George: the pseudonym of Eric Arthur Blair (1903-1950), British journalist and writer, who published his book *1984* two years before his death. In this work he predicted the enormous power of the media that would be expressed through a "Big Brother", a dictator that controlled people's lives. From that character came the idea for the first reality show broadcast by the Endemol production house in Holland. In the year 2000 it arrived in Italy and, like an epidemic, spread to other countries: Germany, Portugal, the United States, the United Kingdom, Spain, Belgium, Sweden and Switzerland. The long, sleepless nights of competitors in all editions of the *Grande Fratello* on Canale 5 in Italy are always accompanied by Nutella.

P

PANE (Bread)

One of the staple foods of mankind, a mixture of flour and water, baked in an oven: always delicious with Nutella. The actress and model Martina Colombari is convinced of it: «I crave for bread and Nutella, hazelnut ice-cream and carrot cake» («Bella», 8 July 2003).

PANICUCCI

Federica: fitness enthusiast and an orange belt in karate, this presenter of many television programmes and Radio Dee Jay admits: «I'm part of the ever-growing group of followers of Nutella by night» («Visto», August 2009).

PARTY

An English word that comes from a French word. Today it has become synonymous with fiesta and is frequently associated with Nutella. It seems that it all started in 1994 at the Roman discothèque New Open Gate on the initiative of an anti-drug group of youngsters. For many years now, on New Year's Eve, the administrators of the town of Alba organize a mega-Nutella Party in the town square at midnight to celebrate the start of the New Year.

PEANUT BUTTER

In the United States, peanut butter is a classic, everyday food. Most American kids are raised on it. The Russian writer Elena Kostioukovitch, in her book *Why Italians Love to Talk about Food* (2006), with a preface by Umberto Eco, writes: «Nutella never allowed American peanut butter to become part of the diet of Italian teenagers and children».

PIZZA

Probably *the* most famous Italian food in the world. But this simple flat bread, seasoned with tomatoes and a little oil, is now enriched with many other ingredients. Many *pizzerie* serve pizzas with Nutella (**photo, below**) and a lot of people appreciate this new variation, like the psychologist Paolo Crepet: «Nutella always takes me back to my childhood; it's a completely Italian product and feels like home. I'm crazy about plain pizza with Nutella spread on it when it's still very hot. It's my favorite snack» («Anna», 14 April 2004).

QUANTITY

In Aristotelian logic "quantity" is the third category and indicates the nature of entities that can be divided into parts. Without going too far, Nutella can give you the right amount of calories, as follows: Nutella spread on a slice of bread (1 oz Nutella, 2 oz wheat bread) with a glass of milk (½ cup) and an apple (4 oz) gives our organism 300-400 calories, approximately 15-20% of our daily requirement. This was demonstrated by a group of nutritionists meeting in Alba for a workshop on breakfasts, with Professor Carlo Agostoni of Milan University («La Stampa», 31 October 2009).

R S

RECIPE

The Italian word is *ricetta*, which is also a medical prescription, but here we mean the list of quantities and ingredients needed to prepare a culinary dish or a drink. Nutella's ingredients are listed on its label, though no one actually knows the exact formula, a secret worth millions of Euros, like the formula for Coca-Cola which is locked away in a safe in Atlanta, U.S.A.

RICCI

Antonio: the author of many television programs and creator of *Striscia la Notizia*, a satirical, daily newscast on Canale 5. Ricci was involved in a quarrel regarding Nutella with writer Ferdinando Camon. In 1993 the latter, in the cultural supplement *Tuttolibri* of «La Stampa», inviting Italians to read more, wrote: «What is that Gabibbo who swallows books as if they were snacks, implying that bookshops are like supermarkets and that books are like Nutella, or a biscuit or yogurt, that you eat, eliminate, and its all over?». He got a reply "signed" by Gabibbo (a big red Muppet-like creature) – but actually written by Antonio Ricci: «… my swallowing books was just a rhetorical device… secondly, I want to state that for me there's more culture in a jar of Nutella than in 80% of the books lying around (and I mean "lying" because they are dead) in any bookshop».

SOCCER

With this colloquial word you have the better-known name for European football, a sport founded in England in 1863 and now played all over the world. In South Africa, where the most recent World Cup was played, in Canada, in the United States, in Australia, in Japan and in other countries, the official name for this sport is soccer. Nutella's involvement in the world of football has always been an intense one: sponsorships for the Champions League, advertising posters in stadiums and the confessions of many a soccer star who admits to stuffing himself with Nutella. For South Africa, Nutella sponsored the Italian national team, using the squad's official cook Silvestri, as well as four young stars of the German national team known as the *jungen Wilden*, the "wild youngsters": Benedikt Höwedes, Mats Hummels, Mesut Özil and Manuel Neuer (**photo, left**).

SORBONNE

Seat of the most famous university in Paris where, at the end of the 1960s the student revolt took place. Occupation of the university occurred again in March 2006, and the French students, like the many Nutella boys in Italy during the 1990s, threw parties and feasts with the Ferrero hazelnut spread.

STREGA

Possibly Italy's most prestigious literary prize. How to win it? It's explained by Maurizio Maggiani, who was awarded the prize in 2005 with his book *Il Viaggiatore Notturno* (The Night Traveler): «a book with a good plot is like Nutella, it nourishes you while you have fun».

T

TARTINUTELLA

The "spreading knife" known as the *TartiNutella* (**photo above, in the hands of a child**), designed by the famous architect Patrick Jouin, was widely acclaimed in France in 2002. It has a wide blade and a groove near the handle that enables you to attach it to the rim of the jar. In 2010 it was displayed at an exhibition dedicated to the French designer at the Pompidou Center in Paris.

TEENAGE

Or, the age of adolescence, to which we would all like to return. In her book *Pizza di Farro alla Rucola con Nutella* (Spelt Flour Pizza with Rocket and Nutella), on the vices of the Italians, the journalist Maria Laura Rodotà describes modern teenagers thus: «... like the adolescents of the previous three generations, they seek consolation eating Nutella on the sly (and sometimes in the dark)».

TENNIS

Whether "forehand" or "backhand" specialists, it seems that many tennis players cannot do without their jar of Nutella. While the Slovak Daniela Hantuchová, who has the physique of a top model, has told «The Times» (13 July 2008) that her favorite dessert is «crêpes with Nutella», the Serbian Ana Ivanovic has confessed to the daily sports newspaper «La Gazzetta dello Sport» (3 May 2009) that «when it comes to eating, ice-cream and Nutella are my weak points», and the Italian Flavia Pennetta has declared («Corriere dello Sport – Stadio», 10 November 2009): «I adore Nutella». But it isn't just beautiful female tennis players who love to "spread". The Spanish champion Rafael Nadal also has spoken of his breakfasts with Nutella every morning («Marca», 6 June 2008).

TOP MODEL

When she becomes one, a woman knows she can ask men for anything. And for herself? What things will she have to give up? Judging from the declarations of many of the most beautiful women in the world, Nutella is not one of them! A backstage reportage at the Milanese fashion shows («Sette» of «Corriere della Sera», 22 July 2010) has revealed some real "surprises" in the apartment shared by a group of top models. First revelation: the models all eat Nutella. Second revelation: the use of multimedia (all the girls have a personal computer with Internet). Third revelation: a "plan B", getting a degree to find a "real" job.

TOTTI

Francesco: the number 10 of the Roma football team has never made a mystery of his predilection. In 2004: «My doping? A jar of Nutella» (Agenzia Ansa, 2 February). Two years later, waking up after a fibula operation he asked for only one thing: a jar of the Ferrero hazelnut spread. «This morning Nutella, but afterwards I shouldn't exaggerate. You'll see, I'm good at controlling myself... » (Ansa, 20 February 2006). An icon of the "Roman" spirit, following another operation in April 2008, Totti received from his fans an exclusive gift: a big jar of Nutella («La Gazzetta dello Sport», 22 March, 2008).

TV

The world is now conditioned by television. Perhaps we should just follow the advice of television author Antonio Ricci: «TV is like Nutella, if you gulp down 4 jars it's bad for you, but if you eat less...» («La Repubblica», 12 March 1996).

U

V

USA

For the 2010 publicity campaign (**below, Times Square; opposite, breakfast with Nutella**) the marketing directors of Ferrero in Somerset invented a new slogan. Instead of «*Che mondo sarebbe senza Nutella*» (What kind of world would it be without Nutella), they decided to be more pragmatic. «Breakfast has never been so good!».

VALERIAN

A medicinal herb with sedative properties, to be consumed either as a herbal infusion or in tablet form. However, some people, like the actress Francesca Neri, have another method: «When I buy Nutella, there are no half measures, but one rule only: no croissants, no bread, no spoon; I eat it with my fingers. It's my own personal ritual: I enjoy it at night, in front of the television, watching a film. It's my way of relaxing before going to sleep. Nutella has virtually become my valerian...» («Anna», 14 April 2004).

VENTURA

Simona: a well-known showgirl and television presenter of sports programs and very popular Italian reality shows, Simona has confessed to the monthly magazine «Flair» (November 2007): «The only snack I can't resist is Nutella».

VOLLEYBALL

This is a sport that requires a great amount of energy. So the Italian women's volleyball team make sure nothing is missing: Simona Gioli told «Elle» (June 2008): «I'm crazy about warm bread with Nutella»; Francesca Piccinini: «I can't say no to Nutella» («Corriere dello Sport – Stadio», 8 November 2009). The amateur player Silvia Battisti, who became Miss Italy in 2007: «Anorexic, no way! I live on pasta and Nutella» («Oggi», October 2007).

W

Z

WINNING ITALY AWARD

Instituted by the Ministry of Foreign Affairs, this prize is an acknowledgement of expressions of Italian excellence, talent and creativity and is awarded to those who have succeeded in promoting and enhancing the image and reputation of Italy in the world. On 5 July 2010 it was awarded to Ferrero: the Italian foreign minister, Franco Frattini, presented the prize at Villa Madama to the brothers Pietro (1963) and Giovanni (1964), the two CEO's of the company who were both born in the years of Nutella's creation.

ZAPPING

An expression used to describe channel surfing on television. Better when done with a jar in your hands, in the evening… as the writer and film-director Bruno Gambarotta claims: «Nutella is loved by a whole generation of thirty to forty-somethings that live "spread out" on well-being, "spread out" on sofas while "zapping", and "spread out" on life» («La Stampa – TuttoLibri», 24 December 1999).

Nutella passion | Letters in a Jar

CHEFS' NUTELLA

Nutella brings people together: in Italy it gathers the family around the breakfast table in the morning, provides both athletes and children with a fun post-game snack, and in the evening stars at parties. Now you will discover that even at the dinner table Nutella offers surprising ideas and inspiration. In the following pages, 40 chefs have each created a gourmet delight featuring Nutella: everything from appetizers, first and main courses, to desserts and ice-cream. Astonish your friends with a complete full-course dinner made with this amazing ingredient.

You'll find Nutella incredibly versatile. Of course, it's wonderful in desserts, but it's also delicious in countless savory dishes. Nutella pairs beautifully with pumpkin to create an unforgettable risotto, adds extra richness to ricotta-filled zucchini flowers, and is magical in polenta. You'll love the savory nutty chocolate hint it adds to meat dishes too. It's a natural in desserts. It can flavor ice-cream, provide a surprising topping for crusty pizza, or even fill sweet agnolotti, a Piedmont classic. It's Nutella's way of bringing different people, ingredients, and tastes together, in a truly "glocal" spirit, that inspires these great chefs to new heights of culinary creativity.

I'm proud of the magnificent team of renowned chefs presented in this new edition of my book. Their wonderful ideas and creative recipes will enable you to prepare innovative, delicious dishes. A nostalgic food, it's no surprise that all the chefs speak of their own childhood or that of their children when thinking about and inviting us to embark on a fantastic gourmet journey with this versatile ingredient that is a part of the collective memory for so many.

VENISON
MEDALLIONS WITH A NUTELLA AND FOIE GRAS CORE

RICCARDO AGOSTINI – IL PIASTRINO (PENNABILLI, PU)

A mouth-watering twist on classic Beef Wellington. Riccardo Agostini smiles: «Nutella is the yummiest thing there is... using it in cooking is fun, as I found out with my friends. We all laughed when, after a while, somebody's little boy couldn't resist any longer and tasted this dish of mine by dipping his finger right in the sauce».

SERVES 4

foie gras	5 slices, about 2 oz each	g 300
venison medallions	4, about 4 oz each	g 500
NUTELLA® spread	4 ½ oz	g 130
kataifi dough	3 ½ oz	g 100
bacon	4 thin slices	g 40
heavy cream	½ cup	cl 10
extra-virgin olive oil		
salt		
black pepper		
vegetable broth		
fresh sage, as garnish, optional		

● Take one slice of the foie gras and pass it through a fine mesh strainer. Blend with 1 ounce of Nutella, season to taste with salt and pepper, and put the mixture into a pastry bag.

● Make a slit in the side of each venison medallion and fill with some of the foie gras/Nutella mixture, reserving a few tablespoons for the sauce. Wrap a slice of bacon around the side of each medallion and tie with kitchen string to maintain its shape.

● Heat a little oil in a sauté pan and sear the medallions on each side. Season to taste with salt and pepper. Degrease the pan, and reserve the pan for making the sauce.

● Preheat the oven to 410 °F. Remove the kitchen string from the medallions and completely wrap them in the kataifi dough. Place the medallions on a baking pan and bake for about 6 minutes, or until the dough is crisp. Remove from the oven and let rest for 2-3 minutes so that the meat juices spread evenly throughout the medallions.

● Meanwhile, using the reserved sauté pan, heat the reserved foie gras/Nutella mixture with a little vegetable broth and stir, mixing until creamy. Reserve.

● In a bowl, beat the heavy cream until stiff peaks form. Fold in the remaining Nutella until just combined to form a mousse. Season to taste with salt and pepper. Reserve.

● In a small dry skillet, sauté the remaining 4 slices of foie gras on each side. Season to taste with salt and pepper.

● Serve by placing the venison medallion and foie gras slice on a serving plate, side by side. Top the foie gras with a quenelle shaped dollop of Nutella mouse and garnish with sage leaves and a drizzle of sauce.

SEMIFREDDO
WITH NUTELLA, SOUR BLACK CHERRIES, CRUNCHY EMMER BREAD AND MOZIA SALT

AIMO AND NADIA – IL LUOGO (MILANO)

From the team of the famous Milanese restaurant, a tongue-in-cheek salty-sweet dessert. To Stefania Moroni that delicious and unmistakable ingredient brings back memories of childhood: «It was the only transgression I was allowed when I was little. No snacks, only wholesome foods. Daddy Aimo and Mommy Nadia only allowed me a treat of bread with olive oil and sugar, or Nutella...».

SERVES 4-6

NUTELLA® spread	2 T	g 40
For the ice-cream:		
heavy cream	½ cup	g 100
granulated sugar	1 T	g 15
egg yolk	1	
vanilla bean from Tahiti		
(just the seeds)	½	
For the sour black cherry gelatin:		
fresh black cherries, pitted	3 ½ oz	g 100
lemon juice	2 drops	
pectin	¼ t	g 1
For the crunchy bread:		
soft part of organic emmer bread		
(naturally leavened)	½ cup	g 50
To garnish:		
fresh black cherries	4	
Mozia salt		

● For the ice-cream: heat the cream to 194 °F. Remove from heat and allow to cool slightly. In a bowl, beat the egg yolk with the sugar and the vanilla until creamy. Slowly drizzle the mixture into the warm cream and stir to combine. Heat over a low flame, stirring constantly, to 149 °F. Remove from heat and allow to cool in the fridge for 2 hours, then pour into an ice-cream maker. After ¾ of the ice-cream making time, add the Nutella to obtain a marbled effect. Finish the ice-cream process.

● Pass the black cherries through a fine mesh strainer and put the purée, along with the pectin, into a saucepan and bring to the boil. Add the lemon juice and immediately remove from heat. Divide the mixture, to a height of ½", between 4 silicone oval molds, approximately 1½"x1". Refrigerate until set, about 2 hours.

● To assemble: use 4 oval molds, 1½"x1". Layer each mold with a ⅓" of the Nutella marbled ice-cream, then a layer of black cherry gelatin and another layer of ice-cream. Place in a blast chiller at 0 °F for an hour.

● Using a sieve, finely crumble the emmer bread, spread onto a baking tray and bake in a 140 °F pre-heated oven for 30 minutes, until crunchy. Allow to cool.

● Unmold the semifreddo carefully onto a dessert plate, and insert a flat wooden "spoon" into each. Sprinkle with the crunchy breadcrumbs, a little Mozia salt and garnish with fresh cherries.

LIDIA'S AGNOLOTTI
WITH NUTELLA

Nutella passion | Chefs' Nutella

LIDIA ALCIATI – RELAIS SAN MAURIZIO, RISTORANTE GUIDO DA COSTIGLIOLE (SANTO STEFANO BELBO, CN)

The famous *agnolòt* from the restaurant *Guido*, but with Nutella. Lidia reveals the "trick" in making them: put the Nutella cream in the fridge before starting the preparation. And she tells us about a happy memory: «Ah, the Nutella: Franca and Michele Ferrero used to come to eat at our restaurant in Costigliole and would bring us a jar, and what a party that was for my children, Piero, Ugo and Andrea».

SERVES 4-6

For the pasta:
NUTELLA® spread	about 12 oz	
all-purpose flour	2 cups	g 250
egg yolks	6	
water	3 T	ml 40-50
semolina flour		

For the sauce:
oranges	4	
sugar	¾ cup	g 200
butter	1 T	

- Refrigerate the Nutella until firm, about 2 hours.
- Make the homemade pasta in the usual way: sift the flour onto a work surface, creating a well in the center. Add the yolks and water to the well and slowly combine in the flour until dough forms. Knead the dough until smooth and silky. Cover with a napkin and leave to rest for 30 minutes.
- After this time take a section of dough and roll it through a pasta machine, starting from the widest setting and finally moving to the thinnest. Once ready, lay the pasta on a work surface and place hazelnut-sized balls of Nutella onto the pasta leaving about 1" between each. Cover with another strip of pasta and using your thumb press down firmly around the filling so that the two layers of pasta adhere. Then "pinch" each individual agnolotto to give it its famous "plin" shape.
- Using a serrated pastry cutter, cut lengthwise through the whole line of agnolotti on both sides of the filling, then, still with the pastry cutter, separate each one.
- Cover a tray with a cotton napkin or cloth and sprinkle with semolina flour. Place the agnolotti onto the napkin and refrigerate until ready to use.
- Prepare the sauce: peel the oranges, taking care not to cut through or remove the white pith. Finely cut the peels and reserve. Bring a large pot of water to the boil and boil the oranges, 5 times, changing the water each time. Once cool, squeeze the juice from the boiled oranges. In a skillet boil the juice with the sugar and the reserved peels, and cook until it becomes a caramelized syrup.
- At this point, cook the agnolotti, taking them directly from the fridge into the boiling water for 90 seconds, drain, and sauté in the pan with the caramelized oranges and butter. Serve hot.

FLAT IRON
BRAISED BEEF AND SLICED GRILLED STEAK WITH PORCINI MUSHROOMS AND POLENTA TARAGNA WITH NUTELLA

LIDIA BASTIANICH AND FORTUNATO NICOTRA – FELIDIA (NEW YORK)

From New York City's *Felidia* restaurant, this reinvention of the polenta of Friuli was inspired by Lidia and created by her executive chef, Fortunato. Lidia's memories of Nutella: «I left Italy before it existed; I found it in the States as an alternative to peanut butter». Fortunato: «My first training sessions at the Colombatto Hotelier Institute in Turin on how to decorate cakes were with Nutella in the pastry pouch, the easiest cream to spread...».

Nutella passion | Chefs' Nutella

SERVES 4

For the braised beef:

a flat iron braising cut	1 ¼ lbs	g 600
stalk of celery	1	
carrot	1	
onion	1	
clove of garlic	2	
sprig of rosemary	1	
concentrated tomato purée	1 T	
dried porcini mushrooms	2 oz	g 50
red wine	½ cup	ml 120
beef broth	2 cups	ml 500
extra-virgin olive oil	4 T	
salt and pepper		

For the polenta taragna:

water	1 cup	ml 250
bay leaf	1	
buckwheat polenta	1 cup	g 100
NUTELLA® spread	4 t	
butter	3 ½ T	g 50
Grana Padano, grated	¼ cup	g 50
salt	1 t	g 5

For the sliced steak:

beef hanger steak	1 lb	g 450
sea salt		
extra-virgin olive oil	3 T	
black pepper		

For the porcini mushrooms:

fresh porcini mushrooms, cleaned and sliced	½ lb	g 200
clove of garlic, crushed	1	
extra-virgin olive oil	2 T	
chopped parsley	2 T	

● For the braised beef: place the dried mushrooms in a small bowl, cover with warm water and leave to soak for 30 minutes. Meantime, clean and finely chop the vegetables.

● In a saucepan, lightly brown the meat in hot oil for 6-7 minutes, add the vegetables and cook for 5-10 minutes, then add the concentrated tomato purée and the drained and squeezed mushrooms, and continue cooking for another 5 minutes. Add the red wine and allow to evaporate, cover with the beef broth, and bake at 350 °F for 2 hours. Remove from oven, remove the meat from the sauce, and cut it into 4 portions.

● Over a high flame reduce the remaining cooking juices until thickened.

● Meanwhile prepare the polenta. In a saucepan combine the water and bay leaf and bring to a boil. Remove the bay leaf, drizzle in the buckwheat polenta and stir occasionally. Allow to cook for 40 minutes. Remove from the heat and whisk in the butter, grated Grana Padano and Nutella. Season to taste with salt.

● For the sliced steak: salt and pepper the beef hanger steak and cook on a very hot grill, 3-4 minutes each side. Let the meat rest, then slice. Season with salt and oil.

● For the porcini mushrooms: in a non-stick pan sauté the mushrooms in the hot olive oil for 2 minutes, add the garlic, salt and parsley, and allow to cook another 2 minutes.

● To serve: spread 2 tablespoonfuls onto each serving plate and top, on one side with a piece of braised beef, and on the other side with several slices of grilled steak. Drizzle with the sauce and top with a spoonful of porcini mushrooms.

NUTELLA
AND BREAD

MASSIMO BOTTURA – OSTERIA LA FRANCESCANA (MODENA)

A creation of *haute cuisine* starring the famed hazelnuts from Piedmont's Langa region. Massimo remembers, with a touch of nostalgia: «As a boy I used to play in the Modena soccer team and a slice of bread and Nutella was our reserve of energy. Now, after a stressful evening at the restaurant I still dip bread sticks into the Nutella jar...».

SERVES 6

For the hazelnut water:
IGP Piemonte hazelnuts, peeled and toasted	1 lb	g 500
sugar	½ cup	g 100
distilled water	2 cups	g 500

To assemble:
NUTELLA® spread	3 ½ oz	g 100
kappa gelatin	¼ t	
soy lecithin	½ t	g 2
organic bread, wood-oven baked	1 slice	

● For the hazelnut water: grind the hazelnuts and sugar in a food processor. Add the water and mix until combined. Pour the mixture into a bowl and let rest at room temperature for 2 days. Strain the mixture, discard the hazelnut solids, reserving the hazelnut water.

● Mix the Nutella with ½ cup of the reserved hazelnut water and pour the mixture in Silpat ravioli molds. Freeze at -4 °F.

● Mix a small amount of the remaining hazelnut water with the kappa gelatin and bring to the boil in a small saucepan. Remove from heat and when the liquid is 122 °F, carefully place the frozen Nutella ravioli in the liquid to defrost them.

● Take the bread, toast it, then place in a mixer with a drop of hazelnut water, and blend.

● For the "hazelnut foam": vigorously whisk a little soy lecithin with some of the reserved hazelnut water.

● To assemble: put some of the bread at the bottom of a classic martini glass, top with hazelnut water and Nutella ravioli. Garnish with the hazelnut froth.

NUTELLA
AND COFFEE ICE-CREAM SUNDAE WITH COCOA NIBS, BRIOCHE CROUTONS AND CANDIED LEMON

JIMMY BRADLEY – RED CAT (NEW YORK)

A sundae is a typical American ice-cream dessert, served topped with sweet sauces, fruit, nuts, and whipped cream. It's generally eaten after a meal or as a snack. Its name comes from "Sunday", because in the 19th century it was traditionally prepared on Sundays. Bradley, who loves Mediterranean cooking and especially Italy, has enriched his sundae with Nutella: «I discovered it in Italy and I've never left it since...».

SERVES 8-10

For the coffee ice-cream:

whole milk	4 cups	l 1
heavy cream	4 cups	l 1
espresso roasted coffee beans	½ lb	g 250
regular roast coffee beans	1 ¼ lb	g 625
egg yolks	27	
granulated sugar	1 ½ cups	g 330
kosher salt	1 T	g 15

For the brioche and cocoa with croutons:

butter (cold, plus more for pan)	8 T	g 125
whole eggs	8	
yeast	1 oz	g 25
granulated sugar	3 oz	g 75
kosher salt	½ oz	g 18
bread flour	5 ½ cups	g 710
toasted cocoa nibs	½ lb	g 250

For the candied lemon:

whole lemons	2	
water	3 cups	ml 750
sugar	1 ½ cups	g 375

For the mascarpone-whipped cream:

heavy cream	2 cups	ml 500
mascarpone cheese	½ lb	g 250
kosher salt	1 t	g 5
acacia honey	2 T	g 45
water	3 cups	ml 750

To complete:

NUTELLA® spread	6 oz	g 180
ripe bananas	2	

●For the coffee ice-cream: with an electric whisk, whisk together the egg yolks and sugar until pale and frothy. Combine the milk, cream, and both coffee beans in a heavy-bottomed saucepan, and heat on low until the mixture almost comes to a boil. Using a hand whisk to stir continuously, slowly pour the milk mixture over the egg mixture.

●Return the combined mixture to the saucepan and stir with a wooden spoon over low heat. Continue to cook until it thickens slightly and coats the back of the spoon. At this point remove from heat and cool immediately by plunging into water and ice. Refrigerate for 12-24 hours: strain, then place into an ice-cream maker, following manufacturer's instructions.

●Prepare the brioche. In a mixer bowl with a dough hook combine the sugar, salt, flour and 6 of the eggs, and knead slowly until blended. Add the 2 remaining eggs and the yeast, and mix until smooth then slowly add the diced cold butter. Continue kneading until the dough starts to pull away from the sides of the bowl. Add the cocoa nibs and continue to mix until fully incorporated. Let the mixture rest, covered with a dish cloth for 1 hour, then refrigerate overnight. Coat the inside of two loaf pans with clarified butter and chill until hardened. Divide the dough evenly between the pans. Cover and let rise by almost double in a warm place.

● Pre-heat the oven to 375 °F. Bake for 15 minutes at that temperature, then reduce the heat and bake at 350 °F for 20 min-

utes, and 320 °F for 15 minutes, until dark brown. Remove from loaf pans and allow to cool completely. With a serrated knife, cut off all the crusts and dice the loaves into ½" cubes. Place the croutons on a buttered baking tray and toast until golden brown.

● Prepare the candied lemon. With the help of a potato peeler or sharp knife, julienne the lemon. In a heavy-bottomed small saucepan, bring the water and sugar to a boil; add the lemon peel and boil for a few minutes. Drain and place on a rack to remove excess sugar and cool.

● For the whipped cream-mascarpone: blend all the ingredients in a large mixing bowl and whisk until thick. Refrigerate until ready to serve.

● In the bottom of each Sundae glass place slices of bananas and a few candied lemon peels. Cover with a spoonful of Nutella (approx 1 ounce), a sprinkling of brioche croutons and two spoonfuls of coffee ice-cream. Repeat the layers until the Sundae glass is full. Top with mascarpone cream.

ROCHER
OF RABBIT LIVER
WITH NUTELLA

TONINO CANNAVACCIUOLO – VILLA CRESPI (ORTA SAN GIULIO, NO)

A nice play on words for this appetizer that imitates a Ferrero chocolate praline. A whimsical recipe which Tonino Cannavacciuolo dedicates to Nutella, that is «the ingredient of childish tantrums and the first thing I ever "stole" from my mother's kitchen. Everyone can afford it now, but when I was a child I was forced to become a Nutella… thief. My mother had said not more than one jar a week, but I was so greedy for it…».

SERVES 6

rabbit livers	½ lb	g 200
butter	9 T	g 120
heavy cream	¼ cup	g 50
gelatin	½ sheet	
NUTELLA® spread	3 T	g 50
salt and pepper		
red port wine	2 T	ml 25
cognac	2 T	ml 25
crushed hazelnuts	½ lb	g 200

● Cut the rabbit livers into cubes: place in a bowl, salt and pepper to taste, and allow to rest for 20 minutes. Sauté the livers in a pan in 1 tablespoon of the butter, over a high flame, then add the port and the cognac and allow to evaporate. Remove from heat and allow to cool.

● Put the gelatin sheet in cold water for 10 minutes, drain, and squeeze out excess water. Reserve. Place the livers in a food processor and blend slowly, adding the cold butter a little at a time. Blend in the cream and finally the gelatin. Refrigerate the mixture for a few hours until firm.

● Using a small melon scoop, make little nut-sized balls from the liver mixture. Using a kitchen syringe, squeeze ½ teaspoonfuls of Nutella into each ball.

● Finally, roll the balls in the crushed hazelnuts until evenly coated. Refrigerate until ready to serve. Serve each on a fluted paper wrapper.

BOAR
IN DOLCEFORTE WITH NUTELLA AND PAPPARDELLE PASTA

CESARE CASELLA – SALUMERIA ROSI (NEW YORK)

Boar in dolceforte sauce is one of the oldest classic Tuscan recipes. Cesare Casella, who has brought his Lucca specialties to New York, has enriched his recipe with Nutella. It's a way of paying homage, so he says, to the "made in Italy" brand: «Nutella is one of the great Italian products, created from the age-old tradition of hazelnut cream, and has gone on to have worldwide success».

SERVES 6

pappardelle	1 lb	g 500
wild boar meat, cubed	2 lbs	kg 1
kosher salt and pepper		
all-purpose flour	2 oz	g 50
extra-virgin olive oil	4 T	
onion, chopped	2	
carrot, chopped	2	
celery stalks, chopped	3	
garlic cloves, chopped	2	
rosemary, chopped	1 sprig	
crushed juniper berries	7	
dry bay leaves	3	
red wine	2 cups	ml 500
meat or vegetable broth	10 cups	ml 2500

For the dolceforte:

toasted pine nuts	2 oz	g 60
raisins		
(soaked in ½ cup red wine)	2 oz	g 60
bitter chocolate, grated	2 oz	g 60
NUTELLA® spread	2 oz	g 60
nutmeg	½ t	
granulated sugar	1 T	
red wine vinegar	2 T	

● Season the meat with salt and pepper, coat with flour, shaking off any excess.

● In a heavy bottomed saucepan, heat the olive oil, add the meat and sauté for 5-7 minutes, stirring frequently until browned on all sides. Add the onions, carrots, celery, garlic, rosemary, bay leaves and juniper berries. Sauté until the onion is translucent. Add the red wine, cover the saucepan, and allow to simmer over a low flame for 30 minutes. Salt and pepper to taste. If the stew dries out, add more broth, a little at a time.

● Add all the dolceforte ingredients to the boar stew and cook for another 30 minutes, adding more broth if necessary. Towards the end of the cooking time, using a hand whisk, blend the sauce, adding 2 cups of broth, and cook for another 15 minutes.

● Cook the pappardelle pasta in abundant salted boiling water, drain when *al dente* and sauté in a pan with the boar dolceforte sauce.

PIZZA
WITH NUTELLA, COARSE SALT, SEA URCHIN AND CLEMENTINE OIL

MORENO CEDRONI – RISTORANTE MADONNINA DEL PESCATORE (SENIGALLIA, AN)

When Moreno Cedroni first became a restaurateur, he also served pizza in his lovely restaurant overlooking the Adriatic Sea. This recipe looks back at those times with a touch of irony, and a surprising flavor combination. A homage to Nutella, which the chef notes, «is part of our collective childhood memories. Even my daughter is now crazy about it and my wife, well even she allows herself a spoonful every now and then».

MAKES 20 APPETIZER-SIZED PIZZAS, ABOUT 1 3/4 OZ (50 G) EACH:

For the pizzas:

all-purpose flour	4 cups	g 500
water	1 cup	g 250
extra-virgin olive oil	1 T	g 15
granulated sugar	½ oz	g 12
salt	½ oz	g 12
brewer's yeast	¾ oz	g 22

For the filling of each pizza:

NUTELLA® spread	2 T	g 50
sea urchin (the flesh)	1	
coarse salt (from Cervia)	a pinch	
clementine olive oil	1 T	g 15

● Knead all the ingredients, until a smooth dough forms, and allow to rise for about 30 minutes. Roll out the dough until very thin, about ⅛" thick. Using a 4" cookie cutter cut out about 20 rounds.

● Put the rounds on a floured surface and allow to rise for another 15 minutes. Prick the entire surface with a fork and bake in a pre-heated oven at 400 °F for 10 minutes until golden.

● Cut each pizza in half and spread each half with Nutella. Add a sea urchin, close the pizza, drizzle with the clementine flavored oil and sprinkle with coarse salt.

CIABATTA
WITH NUTELLA
AND CARAMELIZED BANANA

ENRICO AND ROBERTO CEREA – DA VITTORIO (BRUSAPORTO, BG)

A rich and intriguing dessert, made with *ciabatta*, a bread that has a long-standing tradition in Italy. Enrico and Roberto: «We always have Nutella at home and frequently take to it armed with a spoon. We're very attached to it. Sometimes, when work is over, there can be some sinful transgression with the jar...».

SERVES 4

For the sandwich:
ciabatta loaf	1	
whole milk	1 cup	g 200
NUTELLA® spread	3 ½ oz	g 100
demerara sugar	½ cup	g 100
butter	¼ cup	g 50
egg yolks	2	
banana liqueur	1 cup	ml 200
vanilla rum	1 cup	ml 200
vanilla bean	1	

For the caramelized banana:
banana, not too ripe	1	
granulated sugar	½ cup	g 100
lemon, zest only	1	
orange, juice only	1	
butter	1 T	
vanilla bean	1	

For the banana sherbet:
bananas	3	
sugar syrup	⅔ cup	g 150
lemon juice	½	
grated nutmeg	1 t	

● For the sandwich: with a serrated knife, cut off the crust of the ciabatta to obtain a rectangular piece of bread (about 4½" long, 2½" wide and 1½" thick). Place in the freezer for 15-30 minutes, until the soft part of the bread has hardened slightly.

● Once firm, remove the bread from the freezer and cut it horizontally in half. In the center of each of the two bread halves hollow out a small space not more than ½" deep and fill with Nutella.

● Beat one of the yolks. Brush the outside of the bread with the yolk. Join the two halves together again to re-form the sandwich.

● Simmer the milk with the vanilla bean, then allow to cool. Remove the bean. In a mixing bowl, beat the remaining egg yolk, vanilla-infused milk, banana liqueur and vanilla rum. Dip the sandwich in the mixture, coating it well on all sides. Carefully remove the bread from the mixture using a spatula and place in the freezer for at least 30 minutes, then allow to rest at room temperature for 10-15 minutes.

● Melt the butter in a non-stick pan and fry the sandwich until golden-brown on all sides. Keep warm until ready to serve.

● In a small saucepan allow the demerara sugar to caramelize then pour it over the sandwich.

● For the caramelized banana: peel the banana and cut it in half lengthwise. Reserve. In a small pan heat the sugar until golden and caramelized. Add the butter, vanilla bean, lemon zest and orange juice. Stir the ingredients for a few seconds. Coat the banana halves with the sauce.

● For the banana sherbet: blend the bananas, sugar syrup, lemon juice and nutmeg in a blender until smooth. Place the mixture in the ice-cream maker and follow manufacturer's directions.

● To serve: place the warm sandwich on a plate, cover with caramelized banana, and serve with quenelles of banana sherbet on the side.

HAZELNUT PIE

SALVATORE DE RISO – SALDERISO (MINORI, SA; ROMA)

Salvatore De Riso's tribute to the *Tonda of the Piacenza Hills,* the original IGP Giffoni hazelnut that goes so well with Nutella cream. The Neapolitan pastry chef says: «My daughter, Anastasia, wants to bring the single portion tubs of Nutella to school, as mid-morning snacks... and I recall the long days on the beach when we were kids, playing with my friends. Every one of those days ended with us spreading Nutella on bread».

Nutella passion | Chefs' Nutella

SERVES 8

For the hazelnut short crust pastry:

butter	1 cup	g 240
confectioners' sugar	1 cup	g 160
Giffoni hazelnuts, toasted and ground	½ cup	g 100
egg	1	
egg white	1	
baking powder	1 t	g 4
salt	a pinch	
vanilla bean, Bourbon islands	1	
cake flour	2 ½ cup	g 400

For the hazelnut filling and garnish:

butter	¾ cup	g 150
confectioners' sugar	1 cup	g 150
eggs	3	
Giffoni hazelnuts, ground	¾ cup	g 150
salt	¼ t	g 2
orange zest	½	
NUTELLA® spread	7 oz	g 200
hazelnuts, crushed and toasted, as garnish		

● Beat the butter with the confectioners' sugar until creamy. Mix in the ground hazelnuts and then add the egg, egg white, baking powder, and salt. Grate the vanilla bean with a microplane and add to the batter along with the flour. Mix until just combined. Refrigerate the dough for several hours.

● Prepare the filling: beat the butter with the confectioners' sugar, salt and orange zest. Slowly beat in the eggs and the ground hazelnuts.

● Prepare the pie: preheat the oven to 335 °F. Roll out the dough about ¼" thick. Lay the dough into an 8 to 9" pie pan. Fill with the hazelnut mixture to ¾ full. Bake for about 35 minutes. Allow the pie to cool to room temperature.

● Remove from the pie pan and place on a serving platter. Put the Nutella into a pastry bag and pipe waves across the surface of the pie.

● Garnish the sides with crushed hazelnuts.

MILLEFEUILLE
OF HAZELNUT CREAM AND NUTELLA

GENNARO ESPOSITO AND VITTORIA AIELLO – TORRE DEL SARACINO (MARINA DI SEIANO, VICO EQUENSE, NA)

A twice-toasted, double-hazelnut cream, the aroma enhanced by the Nutella. Gennaro Esposito: «It has become part of everyday family life. The invention of Nutella is as important as Colombus's egg... Personally I prefer savory tastes, but I learned to appreciate Nutella as a boy in my uncle's pastry workshop, in huge 5-kilo jars. Unforgettable».

SERVES 4

For the hazelnut cream (yield: about 1 ¼ cup - 300 g):

Giffoni hazelnuts, blanched and toasted twice	2 ½ oz	g 70
granulated sugar	¼ cup	g 63
egg yolks	2	
milk	1 cup	g 250
cornstarch	4 T	g 35
vanilla bean	1	

For the millefeuille (20 pieces):

confectioners' sugar	⅓ cup	g 50
butter	4 T	g 50
cake flour	½ cup	g 50
egg white	1	
NUTELLA® spread	5 oz	g 150
berries such as strawberries, raspberries, blueberries or blackberries		
confectioners' sugar		

● For the hazelnut cream: place the hazelnuts in a food processor and grind until fine. In a thick-bottomed saucepan whisk the egg yolks with the sugar until smooth, then add the cornstarch, grated vanilla bean and milk. Bring to a boil, stirring constantly with a wooden spoon, until velvety smooth cream. Immediately remove from the heat and allow to cool. Whisk in the ground hazelnuts.

● Prepare the millefeuille: preheat the oven to 400 °F. In a mixing bowl lightly beat the egg white with the confectioners' sugar until smooth. Add the butter and the flour and beat until well blended. Line a baking pan with parchment paper and thinly spread the mixture evenly over the pan, about ¹/₁₀" thick. Cut into rectangles of 1½"x3" and bake for 3-4 minutes. Remove from the oven and allow to cool.

● To assemble: alternate a layer of millefeuille with a layer of hazelnut cream and Nutella spread.

● Garnish with the berries of your choice and a dusting of confectioners' sugar.

SWEET MEMORY
CAKE

GINO FABBRI – PASTICCERIA GINO FABBRI (BOLOGNA)

A cake with the taste of tradition created by the pastry chef Gino Fabbri, who recalls: «Nutella? I was around when it first appeared: everyone liked it immediately and it gets better and better thanks to evolving technologies and high production standards. But if this is my professional opinion, I don't want to forget the gratification it provides at times of depression and the satisfaction for the palate».

SERVES 6

NUTELLA® spread	5 oz	g 150
butter	7 T	g 100
egg yolks	4	g 75
granulated sugar	⅓ cup, plus 2 T	g 100
vanilla bean	1	
egg whites	2	g 50
cake flour	1 cup	g 100
baking powder	1 t	g 8
crushed hazelnuts		
whole hazelnuts		
confectioners' sugar		

● Butter and lightly flour a 8½" cake pan. Preheat the oven to about 330 °F.
● Melt the Nutella and butter in a bowl in the microwave or over a bain-marie, then allow to cool to room temperature.
● In a mixing bowl, thoroughly whisk the egg yolks with ¼ cup of the sugar until light yellow and frothy. Open the vanilla bean and scrape the center into the mixture.
● In a separate mixing bowl, whisk the egg whites with the remaining sugar until stiff peaks form.
● To the egg yolk-sugar mixture add the flour and baking powder, a spoonful at a time, then delicately fold in the stiff egg whites.
● Pour the mixture into the prepared pan and bake for about 30 minutes.
● Remove from the oven and, when cool, unmold onto a serving platter. Dust with confectioners' sugar and garnish with tufts of Nutella and whole hazelnuts.
● If you like, add crushed hazelnuts to the outside edges.

NUTELLA
ICE-CREAM
AND ITS ELEMENTS

GUIDO MARTINETTI AND FEDERICO GROM – GROM (TORINO, NEW YORK, MILANO, BERGAMO, GENOVA, PARMA, PADOVA, FIRENZE)

A recipe from the inventor of a chain of high-quality ice-cream shops, perfect for home ice-cream makers. Guido Martinetti: «As a young man I used to compete in triathlon trials: racing, swimming, cycling. A tough discipline, and when I finished I would reward myself with a Nutella-based snack which I alternated with some pastry-shop gianduia cream. Because "she" is unique, it's a fantastic product with an inimitably appetizing, matchless taste».

Nutella passion | Chefs' Nutella

SERVES 4-6 (yields about 1 lb - 500 g)

whole milk	1 ⅓ cups	g 330
heavy cream	1 ½ T	g 20
NUTELLA® spread	4 oz	g 120
granulated sugar	2 ½ T	g 35
Tonda gentile del Piemonte		
hazelnuts, finely crushed	¾ oz	g 20
dark chocolate, grated	¾ oz	g 20

● Place the milk and the cream together in a heavy-based saucepan and bring almost to a boil (185 °F). Reduce the heat to very low, add first the Nutella and then the sugar, and mix slowly until completely blended. Refrigerate until cold.
● After at least 2 hours pour the cold mixture into an ice-cream maker and follow manufacturers' directions. Just before the ice-cream hardens, stir in the grated chocolate and crushed hazelnuts.

NUTELLA
SOUFFLÉ

IGINIO MASSARI – PASTICCERIA VENETO (BRESCIA)

A classic from the master of masters of Italian pastry chefs, ingenious in its simplicity. Iginio Massari explains: «Nutella has always been the food treat given as a prize, the trophy of our youth. It was born out of the skill of an Italian artisan who had the impeccable intuition of marketing it at exactly the right time. I appreciate the food industry, when it's not just about business».

SERVES 4

NUTELLA® spread	3 ½ oz	g 100
butter	1 ½ T	g 20
salt	a pinch	g 2
egg whites	2	g 50
superfine sugar	1 T	g 15
confectioners' sugar		

● Preheat the oven to 350 °F. Lightly butter 4 individual ramekins or soufflé molds and dust with sugar.
● Allow the butter to soften to room temperature, then whisk it in a bowl until thick and creamy.
● In a separate bowl, using an electric hand-held beater, beat the egg whites and salt until stiff, and then slowly beat in the superfine sugar.
● Add the Nutella to the butter until well blended. Slowly fold the egg whites into the Nutella-butter, a spoonful at a time. Be careful not to deflate the egg whites.
● Divide the mixture among the molds and dust with confectioners' sugar. Bake for 7 minutes. Remove from the oven and serve while still hot.

BRAISED OXTAIL
WITH RADICCHIO AND NUTELLA

TONY MAY AND MATTEO BERGAMINI – SD26 (NEW YORK)

A main course, the meat made even more appetizing by an unusual sauce. Tony May, the great pioneer of Italian cuisine in the United States, has been joined in his restaurant by a young executive chef, Matteo Bergamini: «Nutella is a return to infancy, to when I was a child. Here in the States I've rediscovered it with pleasure, especially with ice-cream, it's been a real joy! Yes, as they say, Nutella is Nutella...».

SERVES 4

oxtails	2	
aged pancetta	3 oz	g 80
vegetable broth	2 cups	ml 500
parsley, minced	1 oz	g 30
sprig of thyme	1	
carrot, minced	1	
onion, minced	½	
clove of garlic, minced	1	
extra-virgin olive oil	½ cup	ml 100
white wine	½ cup	ml 120
concentrated tomato purée	2 T	
celery stalks, finely chopped	2	
raisins	1 oz	g 30
toasted hazelnuts, halved	¾ oz	g 20
NUTELLA® spread	1 ½ oz	g 40
radicchio	1	
salt and pepper		
To garnish:		
crushed hazelnuts	1 T	g 15
cocoa nibs	· 1 T	g 15

● Bone the oxtails and tie with kitchen string to keep each piece together, lightly salt and pepper. Blanche for several seconds in boiling water.

● Dice the pancetta and put into a saucepan, with the parsley, thyme, carrot, onion, garlic and oil. Stir and sauté for a few minutes. Add the meat and sauté until lightly browned; add the white wine and allow it to evaporate. Mix the tomato purée with the hot vegetable broth and add to the saucepan. Cover and cook over a low flame for about 3 hours.

● When cooked, remove the meat and add the celery, raisins, hazelnuts and the Nutella. Mix well and season to taste with salt and pepper.

● Cut the radicchio into slices lengthwise and grill in the oven.

● To serve: on each plate place 2 slices of oxtail covered with the sauce and 2 slices of grilled radicchio. Garnish with fresh celery leaves, a smear of Nutella and a line of chopped hazelnuts and cocoa nibs.

MILLEFEUILLE
OF SMOKED FOIE GRAS
WITH NUTELLA AND CHERRIES

FABRIZIA MEROI – LAITE (SAPPADA, BL)

«I was excited at the idea of creating an unusual savory dish that could be an appetizer or a pre-dessert. Nutella is part of my childhood memories. Nowadays it's my daughter, Elena, who is particularly greedy for one of my Nutella recipes: I make her special omelettes with Nutella and she will eat them at any time of the day».

Nutella passion | Chefs' Nutella

SERVES 4

smoked duck foie gras	½ lb	g 200
NUTELLA® spread	3 T	g 60
granulated sugar	2 oz	g 50

For the cherry compote:
cherries, pitted	¼ lb	g 100
pectin	¾ oz	g 20
sugar	1 oz	g 30

To garnish:
Maldon salt	1 t	g 5

● Slice the foie gras very thinly, using a sharp knife which has been dipped in boiling water.
● Line the inside of a small loaf pan with plastic wrap, leaving enough over the edges to cover the top.
● Line the bottom of the prepared loaf pan with a thin layer of foie gras slices, then, using a spatula spread with a thin layer of Nutella. Continue layering the foie gras and Nutella, finishing with a foie gras layer. Cover the top with plastic wrap, pressing down lightly to combine the layers. Refrigerate for at least 2 hours.
● In the meantime make the cherry compote: in a saucepan, place the pitted cherries and pectin and cook over a high heat for 2 minutes, stirring continuously. Add the sugar and continue stirring for another 3 minutes. Allow to cool to room temperature.
● Remove the foie gras terrine from the fridge, unmold onto a platter, remove the plastic wrap and cut into 4 slices. Place each slice on a small plate, dust with sugar, then caramelize with a pastry torch. Serve with a few spoonfuls of cherry compote and a few grains of Maldon salt.

GLAZED APRICOTS
FILLED WITH NUTELLA

DAVIDE PALLUDA – ENOTECA (CANALE, CN)

The taste of childhood for a recipe with a surprising effect. Davide Palluda confides: «It all started in the 80s, when I was nine years old. I used to spend my summer holidays in a campsite on the Ligurian coast. I played with a kid who used to eat fresh apricots and Nutella for his afternoon snack. I was hooked: since then, every summer, I repeat that delicious ritual».

SERVES 4

ripe, unblemished apricots	12	
NUTELLA® spread	12 t	
apricot purée	5 oz	g 150
gelatin, in sheets	½ t	g 3
lime juice	1 t	
sugar	4 t	g 20
fresh mint	12 leaves	
rustic Italian bread, toasted	12 half slices	

● Blanch the apricots for a few seconds in boiling water, then cool immediately in cold water and ice. Peel delicately and split with a sharp knife to remove the pit. Fill the hollow with Nutella and re-join the two halves. Refrigerate.
● Soak the gelatin sheet in warm water, then drain and squeeze out the excess water. Reserve.
● Warm 2 oz of the apricot purée, lime juice and sugar in a saucepan, then add the gelatin and stir until well combined. Add the remaining purée and stir until blended.
● Remove the apricots from the fridge and cover each one completely with the gelatin mixture. Put them back into the fridge until the glaze has solidified. At this point, dip them once again in the gelatin and return them to the fridge.
● To serve, garnish the apricots with mint leaves and serve with toasted bread.

BITTERSWEET
WITH CRUNCHY NUTELLA

MARCO PARIZZI – PARIZZI (PARMA)

An irresistible dessert inspired by the popular Rocher chocolate, a soft cylinder with a hazelnut heart. Marco Parizzi admits: «For someone as greedy as me, as a child, Nutella exerted a fatal attraction. I used to eat it straight off the knife instead of spreading it on bread. No spoon for me... but to kids nowadays I say: Don't do it!»

SERVES 10

For the chocolate mousse cylinders:

whole milk	½ cup	g 100
heavy cream	2 ½ cups	g 600
dark chocolate (70% cocoa), chopped	1 lb	g 500
dark chocolate (56% cocoa), chopped	½ lb	g 250
butter, at room temperature	1 cup	g 250
rum	2 T	g 25
vanilla bean	1	
gelatin	2 sheets	

For the citrus marmalade:

orange and lemon zests	1 oz	g 30
carrot	1	
orange pulp	1 lb	g 500
lemon pulp	1	
granulated sugar	1 ½ cups	g 325

For the dried fruit garnish:

mixed dried fruits (figs, apricots, dates, etc.)	1 lb	g 500
water	2 cups	g 500
granulated sugar	3 ½ oz	g 100
cinnamon	1 stick	

For the Nutella ganache cream:

NUTELLA® spread	10 ½ oz	g 300
heavy cream	¼ cup	g 50
crushed wafers (paillette feuilletine)	2 oz	g 50

● Put the gelatin in cold water for 10 minutes, until softened, then drain and reserve. Pour the milk, ½ cup of the cream and vanilla bean into a saucepan, put over a hot bain-marie, and stirring, bring it to 176 °F.

● Remove from the heat and add the dark chocolates, rum, butter, and finally the reserved gelatin. Stir until all the ingredients are melted and well combined. Whip the remaining cream until soft peaks form, then fold delicately into the chocolate mixture. Refrigerate for 15-20 minutes until it hardens enough to be molded. At this point make 10 cylinders 3 to 4" high and with a knife make a central hole of about ¼". Place the cylinders in the fridge and leave to harden for at least 4 to 5 hours.

● For the citrus marmalade: peel and chop the carrot, and then process it in a mixer for a few seconds with the orange and lemon zests. Add the orange and lemon pulp and process to combine. Pour the mixture and sugar into a saucepan and boil for 40 minutes until it reaches the consistency of marmalade.

● For the dried fruit garnish: bring the water, sugar and cinnamon to a boil. Add the dried fruit and cook for 2 minutes. Allow to cool to room temperature for at least 1 hour. Remove and discard the cinnamon stick.

● For the Nutella ganache cream: in a small saucepan, blend the Nutella with the cream. Heat to 122 °F to obtain a thick, velvety ganache, and then add the crushed wafers.

● To serve: place a dark chocolate mousse cylinder in the center of each dessert plate and fill the central hollow with the Nutella ganache, allowing it to overflow from the top. Garnish with the citrus marmalade and dried fruit.

BREAD,
PIGEON, NUTELLA AND FOIE GRAS

GIANCARLO PERBELLINI – PERBELLINI (ISOLA RIZZA, VR)

A savory recipe with Nutella. But then, of course, it would have been too easy for "the king of desserts" to create something sweet! For Giancarlo Perbellini the hazelnut cream is an absolute hallmark of quality: «For me it is comparable to a "stamp", a signature that has never left me: when I create a dessert I want it to be as appealing and appetizing as Nutella, it has to have the same intensity...».

SERVES 4

corn meal	¼ cup	g 50
pigeons	4	
reduced veal stock	½ cup	ml 100
chopped shallot	2 T	g 20
duck foie gras	¼ lb	g 100
NUTELLA® spread	1 ½ T	g 25
truffle paste	½ oz	g 15
unsweetened cocoa powder	½ t	g 3
extra-virgin olive oil		
salt and pepper		
white wine		
marsala wine		
reduced red wine		
rosemary	2 sprigs	
sage	a few leaves	
Tuscan bread (if possible cut with a slicing machine)	8 very thin slices	

● Prepare the polenta: bring 1¼ cups of salted water to a low boil and sprinkle in the corn meal, whisking to remove any lumps. Cook for 40 minutes. Reserve.

● Clean the pigeons: with a sharp knife remove the thighs then cut through the sternum; open the birds, and carefully remove their insides and de-bone the breasts. Stew the carcasses for stock, and reserve. Season the thighs with salt, pepper, oil and rosemary. Place in a baking pan and cook in a pre-heated oven at 325 °F for 20 minutes, then bone and chop the meat. Clean the livers, the hearts and the stomachs (previously opened and washed) and dice.

● Prepare a meat sauce: in a saucepan with a little olive oil, lightly brown the shallot, add the pigeon interiors (not the livers) and then add the previously cooked and cubed thigh meat. Sauté, then add the white wine, the Marsala wine and a few drops of reduced red wine, a sprig of rosemary and the sage leaves.

● Meanwhile, in a pan, with a little oil, sauté the livers, drain their fat and add to the prepared meat sauce. Add the veal stock and continue cooking for 10 minutes.

● Season the pigeon breasts with salt and pepper, sauté in a pan with hot oil until both sides are browned. Allow to cool for 5 minutes, then cut into thin slices.

● Press the raw foie gras through a fine mesh sieve, collect in a small bowl and mix in the Nutella, truffle paste and cocoa. Salt and pepper to taste.

● To serve. Fry the bread slices in a little oil until crisp, and place 2 slices of bread on each serving plate. Spread each slice with a little liver, Nutella, and top with thin slices of pigeon breast glazed with the stock made from the carcasses.

● Accompany the pigeon with a froth of polenta, using a kitchen siphon, and two spoonfuls of pigeon meat sauce.

NUTELLA
CHOCOLATE, LICORICE AND EXOTIC FRUIT

VALERIA PICCINI – CAINO (MONTEMERANO, GR)

A multi-textured elegant and refined dessert. Valeria Piccini has sweet memories: «On winter evenings when the days get short, we've made a habit, at the restaurant, of eating all together at 6:30 p.m., before the clients start arriving. Then, at midnight, we sometimes get the urge to snack on toasted brioche bread spread with Nutella...».

SERVES 6

For the paillette feuilletine biscuits:

all-purpose flour	2 T	g 30
sugar	2 T	g 30
whole milk	½ cup	g 125
butter	1 oz	g 30
egg	1	
salt	1 t	g 5
vanilla bean	½	

For the crunchy base:

hazelnut brittle	¼ lb	g 125
NUTELLA® spread	4 ½ oz	g 125
milk chocolate (40% cocoa)	¼ lb	g 125
paillette feuilletine	¼ lb	g 125

For the mousse:

granulated sugar	⅓ cup	g 65
water	2 T	g 25
egg yolks	10	g 175
milk chocolate (40% cocoa)	2 ½ oz	g 75
dark chocolate (70% cocoa)	½ lb	g 220
butter, melted	⅓ cup	g 65
whipped cream	1 ¼ cup	g 300

For the exotic fruit sherbet:

passion fruit juice	½ cup	g 100
orange juice	½ cup	g 100
carrot juice	½ cup	g 100
lemon juice	¼ cup	g 50
granulated sugar	⅓ cup	g 75
glucose	⅓ cup	g 75
white wine	¼ cup	g 50

vanilla bean		½
red chili pepper		½
star anise		3

For the licorice sauce:

granulated sugar	½ cup	g 100
glucose	2 T	g 20
water	¼ cup	g 50
licorice powder	2 t	g 10
cocoa powder	1 ½ t	g 8

For the streusel of almonds and cocoa:

butter	2 T	g 25
all-purpose flour	1 oz	g 25
granulated sugar	1 oz	g 25
almond flour	1 oz	g 25
cocoa powder	2 ½ t	g 12

● Prepare the paillette feuilletine biscuits: heat the milk with the butter, then allow to cool. Separately, in a mixing bowl, prepare the batter: hand whisk the egg, sugar, flour, salt, vanilla seeds and then slowly trickle in the cooled milk-butter mixture.
● Preheat the oven to 335 °F. Lightly butter a 10"x14" rectangular baking pan. Pour a small ladleful of the batter into the pan and bake for 15 minutes. Remove the crêpe from the pan and repeat with the remaining batter. Lay the crêpes on a work surface and cut out rectangles 2"x4". Roll them, place on a baking pan, and return to the oven to dry for 10 minutes at 250 °F.
● Prepare the crunchy base: chop the milk chocolate and melt over a warm bain-marie. Allow to cool slightly and then add in the crushed hazelnut brittle, Nutella and crushed paillette feuilletine. Spread the mixture on the bottom of a pie dish, about ¼" thick, and refrigerate for at least an hour.
● For the mousse: prepare a sugar syrup: pour the water and the sugar into a small saucepan and stir continuously over low

heat until it reaches 250 °F. Whisk it onto the egg yolks, in a slow trickle, and beat for a few minutes.

● To the side, melt the chopped milk chocolate, chopped dark chocolate and butter over a warm bain-marie. Allow to cool and then add to the whisked egg yolks. Delicately fold in the whipped cream. Spread this mousse over the crunchy base and refrigerate for at least 3 hours. Then slice the cake into 2"x2" pieces.

● Prepare the sherbet: put all the ingredients together in a large saucepan, cook over a low heat and stir until the sugar has melted. Filter, allow to cool, and then place in an ice-cream maker following manufacturer's instructions.

● For the licorice sauce, slowly caramelize the sugar and the glucose. To the side, blend into the water the licorice and cocoa powders, then slowly drizzle onto the caramel, stirring constantly until blended and a sauce forms.

● For the streusel: preheat the oven to 320 °F. Using your hands, mix together the flour, almond flour, softened butter and sugar. Place the dough on a Silpat lined pan and bake for 20 minutes. Remove from the oven and, once cool, crumble evenly and dust with cocoa.

● To serve: pour the licorice sauce into a small squeeze bottle and form two parallel lines of sauce across the plate. Top with 2 pieces of crunchy base and chocolate mousse and garnish with a sprinkling of streusel around the plate. Add a few small quenelles of sherbet to the side.

SMILE

GIOVANNI PINA – PASTICCERIA PINA (TRESCORE BALNEARIO, BG)

This cake's amazingly varied textures will make you smile. The pastry chef Gianni Pina has a family anecdote: «My two daughters sometimes snack on bread and Nutella. Since their father is a pastry chef... they eat only cookies and cakes from the family workshop. But Nutella is always in the pantry; I couldn't take that pleasure away from my kids».

SERVES 6

For the flourless cocoa sponge:

egg whites	4	g 120
granulated sugar	⅔ cup	g 160
egg yolks	6	g 100
cocoa powder	2 oz	g 50

For the light milk chocolate cream with Nutella:

heavy cream	½ cup	g 100
NUTELLA® spread	2 ½ T	g 50
milk chocolate	2 oz	g 50
gelatin	2 t	g 10

For the chocolate chips:

dark chocolate (70% cocoa)	2 ½ oz	g 70

● For the sponge cake: preheat the oven to 335 °F. In a mixing bowl, whisk the egg whites with ⅓ cup of the sugar until stiff. In a separate bowl beat the egg yolks with the remaining ⅓ of sugar and then fold with the egg whites. Finally add the cocoa, folding delicately, and then using a pastry sleeve, make two discs 7" in diameter and ⅛" thick. Bake for 15 minutes. Reserve.

● Soften the gelatin sheets in cold water. Heat the cream in a heavy-bottomed saucepan to 140 °F and then blend in the Nutella, chocolate, and softened gelatin. Using an immersion mixer, blend all the ingredients. Line the base of a 7" cake pan with plastic wrap and pour in ¼ cup of the mixture. Refrigerate for 2 hours, until firm.

● Pour the remaining cream mixture into a mixing bowl, cover with plastic wrap and refrigerate for 2 hours, until firm.

● For the chocolate chips. With a knife, chop the dark chocolate very finely, so it resembles grains of rice. Sift the chocolate chips to eliminate any powdered chocolate that may have formed.

● On the base of a 7" spring-form cake pan, place a disc of the reserved sponge cake. Top with the firm disc of reserved milk chocolate cream with Nutella. Sprinkle with the chocolate chips and cover with the second sponge disc. With a hand-held electric mixer or whisk, beat the remaining cold cream-Nutella mixture until frothy and pour into the cake pan. Smooth carefully with the back of a spoon.

● Refrigerate for at least an hour, until firm. Remove the spring-form and decorate, if you like. Serve cold.

NUTELLA
SEMIFREDDO

VITO POLOSA – AROMA KITCHEN & WINEBAR (NEW YORK)

A rich dessert with an inviting presentation. Vito Polosa tells us, with nostalgic irony, of his childhood in Basilicata: «For breakfast I was allowed half a slice of bread with just a smear of Nutella on it... then my mother would lock the jar away. When she had friends visiting and was distracted, I was able to find the key and then "steal" an extra ration. But she caught me once... to say she was angry is an "understatement"...».

SERVES 6

For the semifreddo:
heavy cream	2 ½ cups	ml 590
egg yolks	6	
granulated sugar	½ cup	g 100
NUTELLA® spread	3 t	

For the walnut cookies:
all-purpose flour	2 ½ oz	g 70
butter, softened	⅓ cup	g 75
granulated sugar	2 ½ oz	g 75
walnuts, chopped	2 oz	g 50
baking powder	1 t	g 7
egg yolks	2	

To garnish:
ricotta cheese	½ lb	g 200
granulated sugar	2 oz	g 50

To decorate:
amaretti cookies	¼ lb	g 100
gianduia chocolate bar, chopped	3 ½ oz	g 100

● Prepare the semifreddo: in a large bowl whisk the cream with half the sugar until stiff peaks form. In another bowl, using an electric beater, beat the eggs with the remaining sugar until pale and frothy. Delicately, using a spatula, fold the whipped cream into the egg yolk mixture. Slowly add the 3 teaspoons of Nutella. Blend with a light, slow rotatory movement, from bottom to top so the mixture doesn't deflate, then divide into 6 silicon molds 2" in diameter and 1½" high. Place in the freezer for about 4 hours.

● Prepare the walnut cookies: sift the flour with the baking powder, and reserve. In a mixing bowl, using an electric beater, beat the egg yolks and sugar for 5 minutes, and then incorporate, one at a time, the softened butter, flour, baking powder and finally the finely chopped walnuts. With the help of a rolling pin, spread the dough on a piece of parchment paper or a Silpat, to a thickness of about ¼". Cut out 6 discs, using a pastry cutter 2" in diameter and another 6 discs using a pastry cutter of 2½". Refrigerate for an hour, and pre-heat the oven to 320 °F. Bake for 10-12 minutes.

● In a food processor grind the amaretti until almost a powder. In a bowl, using a whisk, beat the ricotta and sugar for a few minutes. Melt the chocolate over a hot bain-marie, stirring continuously.

● A few minutes before serving the dessert, place a walnut cookie to one side of the serving plate, top with semifreddo and then cover with another walnut cookie. On the other side of the plate, carefully place a quenelle of ricotta, decorated with lines of melted chocolate. Finally, in the center create a subtle wave of amaretti powder.

NUTELLA
SANDWICHES WITH TANGERINE JELLY, SZECHWAN PEPPER AND SAFFRON YOGURT CREAM

NICOLA AND PIERLUIGI PORTINARI – LA PECA (LONIGO, MI)

The Portinari brothers have created a dessert inspired by the old classic, bread and Nutella, with an exotic note. They tell us: «Even now both of us, in our forties, will still eat Nutella straight from the jar by the spoonful. And then there's a way to eat Nutella that the whole family loves; on top of pizza when we eat out».

SERVES 4

For the sandwiches:

white, crustless, sandwich bread	1 package	
heavy cream	1 cup	g 250
NUTELLA® spread	9 oz	g 250
egg, whole	1	
egg yolks	2	
granulated sugar		

For the tangerine jelly:

freshly squeezed tangerine juice	¾ cup	g 200
granulated sugar	¾ oz	g 20
Szechwan peppercorns	10	
tangerine peel	1	
gelatin	2 sheets	g 3

For the yogurt and saffron cream:

plain European-style yogurt	1 cup	g 250
heavy cream	½ cup	g 100
granulated sugar	½ cup	g 100
egg yolks	4	
saffron filaments	10	

● For the sandwiches: in a mixing bowl, whisk the cream, Nutella, egg and yolks. Place the mixture in the freezer to cool for 30 minutes. Line an 8"x8"x1½" baking pan with plastic wrap so that the ingredients don't touch the baking dish.

● Line the bottom of the dish with a layer of the bread then, carefully spread with the cold Nutella mixture. Top with another layer of bread.

● Cover with plastic wrap. Steam cook at 194 °F for about an hour (the cake must be compact). Refrigerate for about 3 hours until cold. Remove the plastic wrap, cut into triangular slices, dust with granulated sugar and toast under a hot grill on both sides until the sugar is caramelized.

● In a small saucepan, combine the tangerine juice and sugar, and heat to 122 °F. Remove from heat, add the peppercorns and tangerine peel, and let steep for 1 hour. Then strain the juice, and slowly warm it until tepid, about 104 °F, and add the gelatin (previously softened in cold water then drained and squeezed) and allow to melt completely. Pour the mixture in a round mold ¾" high and refrigerate until firm.

● Meanwhile prepare the yogurt and saffron cream: mix the ingredients together with a whisk and cook as if it were a custard, at 185 °F, stirring continuously with a spatula.

● To serve, cut the cake into slices, place one slice, cut into triangles, on each dessert plate, and garnish with the tangerine jelly and saffron-yogurt cream.

ZUCCHINI FLOWERS
STUFFED WITH RICOTTA AND NUTELLA
IN A WARM RUM SAUCE

ANTONELLA RICCI – AL FORNELLO DA RICCI (CEGLIE MESSAPICA, BR)

A sweet-savory appetizer which is fresh and tasty. Antonella Ricci has a very clear memory of Nutella, when she began helping her father Angelo and her mother Dora in the family trattoria: «For me Nutella was "the" party, the only way I could get near to chocolate... when I was a little girl. And now my two little girls ask me for Nutella with the same eager greediness».

Chefs' Nutella

Nutella passion

SERVES 4

zucchini flowers	8	
cow's milk ricotta cheese	5 ½ oz	g 150
NUTELLA® spread	2 T	g 30
puffed rice cereal	2 T	g 20
eggs	2	
bread crumbs	½ lb	g 200
almond slices	1 oz	g 30
extra-virgin olive oil	1 qt	l 1

For the sauce:

NUTELLA® spread	3 T	g 50
heavy cream	1 T	g 10
rum	1 T	g 10
salt		

To decorate:

mint leaves	4 sprigs
confectioners' sugar	

● Remove the zucchini flower stalks and wash quickly under a drizzle of water. Dry delicately with a tea towel. Open the leaves gently and take out the central pistils. Allow to dry completely, upside down, over paper towels.

● Strain the ricotta and mix with the Nutella and puffed rice. Place the mixture in a pastry sleeve and stuff the zucchini flowers, being sure to carefully close the petals. Beat the eggs in a small bowl, and combine the bread crumbs and almond slices in another bowl. Dip the filled zucchini flowers first into the beaten eggs and then into the bread crumb mixture. In a large frying pan, heat the oil to 350 °F and fry the zucchini flowers until golden. Remove from the pan with a skimmer and place on double sheets of paper towels.

● For the sauce: mix all the ingredients in a small, deep-bottomed saucepan, and heat over a bain-marie stirring until it reaches a creamy consistency.

● To serve: pour 2 tablespoons of the warm sauce on each serving plate, top with 2 crispy zucchini flowers, dust with confectioners' sugar and garnish with mint.

NUTELLA
PIADINA

ROBERTO RINALDINI – PASTICCERIA RINALDINI (RIMINI)

The traditional flat bread, or *piadina*, from the Romagna area, filled with soft Nutella cream, prepared by the famous young ice-cream and pastry chef. Roberto remembers: «In the courtyard of the house where I lived as a boy, one of my aunts used to pass me Nutella and bread from the balcony when I was playing with my friends. Nutella has always stayed a habit for those of us who have been athletes, a quick supply of energy».

SERVES 4

For the piadina:

all-purpose flour	4 cups	g 500
cocoa powder	½ oz	g 15
NUTELLA® spread	1 T	g 15
granulated sugar	1 t	g 5
salt	2 t	g 10
extra-virgin olive oil	½ cup	ml 130
water	¾ cup	ml 200
baking powder	1 t	g 5

For the filling:

NUTELLA® spread	7 oz	g 200
strawberries, hulled and sliced	5 oz	g 150

● On a work surface, sift the flour, baking powder and cocoa in a mound. Mix with a little of the water and add the remaining ingredients, kneading until blended and smooth. Cover with a kitchen towel and let rest for 30 minutes. Then pinch off about 3 oz of dough at a time, and roll into small balls. Using a rolling pin, flatten each disc until approx 10" in diameter.

● In the Romagna Riviera, at this point, the piadine are cooked on a special smooth round griddle that can be heated over a flame. At home one can use an iron skillet or special crêpe pan. Cook 1 minute per side, keeping the heat constant and piercing with a fork to avoid burning.

● To assemble: place a piadina on a cutting board, spread with a layer of Nutella and scatter with strawberries, then cover with another hot piadina. Cut into triangular slices and serve immediately, right from the cutting board.

NUTELLA,
BREAD AND FENNEL

NIKO ROMITO – REALE (RIVISONDOLI, AQ)

A "dessert that's not a dessert" by this talented chef from Abruzzo, who aims for luxurious simplicity in his cooking. Here the fennel adds an unusual freshness. Niko remembers: «Our Nutella ritual was acted out on Sunday nights. My sisters and I would sit around the table... our mother would come in holding the Nutella jar and the bread. For us it was like seeing a treasure, a diamond».

SERVES 4

fennel, cleaned and chopped	1 lb	g 400
whole milk	3 ¼ cups	g 800
heavy cream	½ cup	g 100
granulated sugar	½ cup	g 140
honey	1 ½ oz	g 40
NUTELLA® spread	14 oz	g 400
water	1 cup	g 250
cinnamon	½ stick	
ground star anise	¼ t	g 1
day-old bread, wood-oven baked	10 oz	g 300
confectioners' sugar		

To garnish:
chocolate wafers and dried fruits

● Put the fennel into a large mixing bowl. Boil the milk, and pour it over the fennel and let steep for 12 hours in a cool place.

● After this time, strain the fennel scented milk. In a small saucepan, over a very low flame, heat the cream, sugar, and honey stirring with a wooden spoon until completely blended. To this mixture, add the strained fennel-infused milk, mix well, and pour into an ice-cream maker.
● Bring the water to the boil with the cinnamon and star anise, remove from the heat and allow to steep for several hours.
● When cool, slowly add the Nutella, a little at a time, until blended to a syrupy consistency.

● Cut the bread into rectangular slices about ¼" thick. Toast the slices on a very hot grill and then dust with confectioners' sugar, and oven-grill them. Dip the bread into the Nutella mixture.
● To serve: divide the Nutella mixture between 4 serving bowls, then top with a slice of the Nutella-dipped toasts and a scoop of ice-cream. Garnish the plate with a chocolate wafer and caramelized dried fruit.

BREAD
AND NUTELLA

ALFREDO RUSSO – DOLCE STIL NOVO ALLA REGGIA (VENARIA, TO)

In this dish, Nutella is served warm with a hint of saltiness. Alfredo Russo explains: «The recipe is inspired by the bread and Nutella of childhood memories, my grandmother's voice calling me upstairs from the courtyard for a snack, after playing with my friends in the afternoon. Even my daughter Carlotta can't do without Nutella, even though our restaurant has numerous desserts to offer».

SERVES 4

For the Nutella sauce:
NUTELLA® spread	5 oz	g 150
whole milk	1 ¾ cups	g 450

For the peanut cream:
salted peanuts, toasted	¼ lb	g 100

For the orange sherbet:
blood oranges	4	
tangerines	2	
lemon	1	
sugar	⅓ cup	g 80
glucose syrup	2 T	g 20

rustic bread		
Modena balsamic vinegar		
extra-virgin olive oil	1 T	
coarse salt	a pinch	

● Place the peanuts in a silicon mold and barely cover with a little water. Place in the freezer and freeze for at least 2 hours, until it becomes a block of ice.

● Prepare the orange sherbet: mix the sugar and the glucose with the citrus juice and refrigerate for 2 hours. After this time, place in an ice-cream maker and follow manufacturer's directions.

● Warm the milk, then mix in a blender with the Nutella, and let rest for 40 minutes. Turn out the peanut-ice block and grate it with a vegetable grater. Collect the dense, smooth purée in a bowl (or use a professional Pacojet instead).

● To serve, cut the bread into small cubes, and toast in a non-stick pan with a few drops of extra-virgin olive oil and a few grains of coarse salt. In individual deep dessert bowls, place the toasted bread cubes, cover with a quenelle of sherbet garnished with a few drops of balsamic vinegar and, to the side, a spoonful of peanut cream. Serve the warm Nutella sauce in a small sauce boat on the side.

CLAFOUTIS
WITH PEARS AND NUTELLA

Nutella passion | Chefs' Nutella

PAOLO SACCHETTI – PASTICCERIA CAFFÈ NUOVO MONDO (PRATO)

A traditional French dessert by a Tuscan pastry chef. Paolo Sacchetti confesses: «I was the family favorite as a child so I could spread Nutella on bread as much as I wanted! Now my son Andrea sends me a special signal when he eats Nutella: it's the only time he likes bread».

SERVES 6

William or Barlett pears, ripe	2	g 180 (each)
NUTELLA® spread	6 oz	g 180
For the pastry:		
confectioners' sugar	4 T	g 50
butter	⅓ cup	g 75
all-purpose flour	1 cup	g 120
egg yolk	1	
vanilla bean	½	
orange zest	1	
salt	a pinch	
For the filling:		
whole eggs	2	
granulated sugar	⅓ cup	g 80
heavy cream	1 cup	g 250

● Mix the butter and confectioners' sugar for a few moments, then add the salt, vanilla and orange zest. Add the egg yolk and blend well, then delicately sift in the flour, a little at a time, and knead the dough until just blended. Make a ball and cover in plastic wrap.

● Refrigerate overnight to infuse the ingredients. Roll out the dough into a 9" pie pan.

● Peel and slice the pears and place on the dough in a fan shape.

● For the filling: beat the eggs with the sugar, then add the cream, and whisk to combine. Pour the mixture over the pears, to the top of the pie pan. Bake in a pre-heated oven at 350 °F for about 30 minutes.

● Remove from the oven, and when still warm, spread the Nutella over the pie.

SOFT AND CRUNCHY
IN A GLASS

VITTORIO SANTORO – CAST ALIMENTI (BRESCIA)

The hazelnut brittle has a slightly salty tang that makes this dessert absolutely unique, a *haute patisserie* created by the director of *Cast Alimenti*. Vittorio Santoro shares a thought: «For the children in our family it was a Sunday special. Our family was made up of five boys and a girl: Nutella made it a real party, with Apulian bread, an unforgettable fragrance».

SERVES 10

For the Italian meringue:

water	¼ cup	g 45
sugar	5 oz	g 150
egg whites	3	g 90

For the mascarpone mousse:

mascarpone cheese	½ lb	g 250
softly whipped cream	⅔ cup	g 150

For the chestnut and Nutella truffles:

marrons glacés (washed under running water, dried, and puréed with a vegetable mill)	¼ lb	g 125
softened butter	1 oz	g 30
NUTELLA® spread	2 T	g 40
cognac XO	1 T	g 15

For the Nutella cream:

custard (see recipe in the text)	1 ¼ cups	g 300
softly whipped cream	1 cup	g 250
NUTELLA® spread	6 oz	g 170
gelatin, in sheets	½ oz	g 10

For the hazelnut caramel:

salt	2 T	g 25
egg whites	1 ½ T	g 20
crushed blanched hazelnuts, toasted	½ lb	g 250
butter	1 oz	g 20
sugar	1 cup	g 250
glucose	¾ cup	g 200

● Prepare an Italian meringue: beat the egg whites until stiff. Heat the water and sugar to 250 °F, then drizzle onto the whites. Very slowly whisk until cool.

● For the mascarpone mousse: beat the mascarpone, then add alternate spoonfuls of the Italian meringue and whipped cream. Refrigerate until ready to use.

● For the chestnut-Nutella truffles: mix the cognac, chestnut purée, softened butter and Nutella, until smooth and of medium consistency. Refrigerate until firm, and then make little truffles about ¼ teaspoon in size.

● For the Nutella cream: prepare a custard with 1 ½ cups cream, ⅔ cup milk, ⅔ cup egg yolks, ⅓ cup sugar and a ¼ of vanilla pod. Boil the cream and the milk together with the vanilla. Beat the egg yolks with the sugar until pale, add to the cream and milk and heat to 185 °F stirring with a whisk over the flame. Soak the gelatin then drain and squeeze, and add it to the warm custard. Add the Nutella and the softly whipped cream and blend gently.

● For the hazelnut caramel: put the hazelnuts into a large mixing bowl and blend with the egg whites and salt. Leave to dry by pouring the mixture onto a baking tray and place in the oven at 122 °F overnight or at 230 °F for an hour. Make the caramel, without any water, just the sugar and the glucose, by letting them melt over a low heat and stirring from time to time. Mix the toasted hazelnuts into the light golden liquid caramel. Mix over the heat until the color is medium dark golden and pour the caramel on a silicon sheet or on a slab of buttered marble, about ¼" thick. When cold, break into medium-small pieces.

● Fill an average-sized glass tumbler half way with a layer of mascarpone mousse then top with crumbled caramel and a few of the truffles. Pour the Nutella cream to almost fill the tumbler. Sprinkle with the remaining crumbled caramel.

TOAST
WITH NUTELLA AND TOMATO (MÈC COMBAL)

BARBARA AND DAVIDE SCABIN – COMBAL.ZERO (RIVOLI, TO)

In this recipe created by the Scabin siblings, the tartness of the tomatoes contrasts with the sweetness of the parfait. Davide: «I personally love a particular way of enjoying Nutella, I make myself a kind of "millefeuille" with salted crackers spread with Nutella, then I dip them into coffee and milk for breakfast. It's a dream». Barbara: «It's delicious in so many ways, for instance, spread on cold polenta made the day before».

SERVES 4

For the parfait:

NUTELLA® spread	9 oz	g 250
egg whites	2	g 60
granulated sugar	⅓ cup	g 100
heavy cream	¼ cup	g 50

For the toasted bread:

sandwich bread	4 slices
extra-virgin olive oil	
coarse salt	a pinch
ground black pepper	a pinch

For the tomato, orange and basil sauce:

medium tomatoes (Porto Palo or Pachino)	2-3	
filtered orange juice	3 T	g 30
extra-virgin olive oil (not too strong tasting)		
fresh basil	4 leaves	
salt		
ground black pepper		

● Combine the egg white and sugar, and heat over a bain-marie to 140 °F, and then beat in an electric mixer until cooled (about 86 °F); this is the meringue base.

● Melt the Nutella in a microwave or over a bain-marie to 86 °F and then fold in the lightly whipped cream.

● Combine the two mixtures, blending delicately with a spatula. Line four molds (size 2½" in diameter and 1" high) with parchment paper (or acetate) and fill them with the parfait mixture. Cool immediately at 0 °F.

● Remember, before serving, to leave at room temperature for a few minutes.

● Meanwhile, prepare the white sandwich bread by removing all the crusts and with a pastry cutter, cut out circles 2½" in diameter (the same as the parfait molds). Sauté each slice of bread in a hot pan with a little extra-virgin olive oil, then season with salt and pepper to taste.

● Wash and cut the tomatoes in half. With a teaspoon, scoop out the seeds and the internal liquid and place in a bowl. Add the filtered orange juice and two of the basil leaves, roughly shredded by hand. To season, mix with a little salt, pepper and extra-virgin olive oil and add a little sugar to balance the acidity.

● Turn out the parfait and place between two discs of bread while still hot, pour 2 tablespoons of the tomato sauce into the center of a deep plate, place the Nutella and toasted bread in the middle, garnish with the remaining sauce, sprinkle with julienne basil leaves and serve immediately.

NUTELLA
WITH BREAD STICKS

EMANUELE SCARELLO – AGLI AMICI (FRAZIONE GODIA, UDINE)

On the outside an envelope of Nutella, on the inside the *grissini*, bread sticks. The chef Emanuele Scarello: «We grew up with *grissini* and Nutella. Sometimes, even now, there are evenings when I have to eat it with a spoon. My wife, Flavia, when pregnant, just couldn't resist Nutella. She used to say: "You'll see, the baby will be born with a craving for Nutella!" And so it was».

SERVES 4

NUTELLA® spread	10 ½ oz	g 300
water	⅔ cup	g 150
agar-agar	½ t	g 3
Turin breadsticks, crushed	8	
extra-virgin olive oil	1 cup	g 250
soy lecithin	½ t	g 2
salt		

● Put the agar-agar in the water and heat to 185 °F, then add the Nutella and bring to a boil. Pour the mixture in a very thin layer onto a baking pan. Allow to cool.

● Cut the "ravioli" with a round pastry cutter 2½" in diameter, place a small amount of crushed breadstick crumbs in the center of each, and seal the ravioli. Heat the oil, add the soy lecithin and whisk to a froth.

● To serve, place 3 ravioli in the center of each plate, topped with a spoonful of oil froth and a sprinkle of salt.

WAFER
OF DUCK FOIE GRAS AND NUTELLA WITH A SHOT OF KIR ROYAL

MAURO ULIASSI – ULIASSI CUCINA DI MARE (SENIGALLIA, AN)

An original *amuse-bouche* presented by a whimsical and innovative chef who recommends that the wafer must be enjoyed by drinking the cocktail down all in one go. Mauro Uliassi recalls the times of his youth: «It was almost an erotic ritual: after the clubs, late into the night, we'd go to the beach and spread... Nutella! Now I only eat it on crackers and I've stopped counting the spoonfuls».

SERVES 15

hazelnut butter	2 oz	g 50
NUTELLA® spread	1 ½ T	g 25
hazelnut candy	1 oz	g 25
butter	1 oz	g 25
duck foie-gras	½ lb	g 200
white truffle oil	1 T	g 10
sheets of wafer		
salt		
balsamic vinegar		
Maldon salt		

For each Kir Royal:

champagne	2 fl. oz	cl 2
Cassis	3 drops	

● Sauté the duck foie-gras in a pan and then purée in a blender along with the Nutella, hazelnut candy, hazelnut butter, truffle oil, and salt and pepper to taste; then pass through a fine mesh sieve.
● Whisk the mixture in a bain-marie over ice, using an immersion mixer, then pour it into a rectangular mold measuring 10"x6½" and ¼" high. Put in the freezer.
● Meantime, cut the wafers (you can find them in professional pastry distributors/stores) into 1"x2" rectangles.
● Remove the frozen mixture and cut it into the same size as the wafers.
● To assemble: layer 3 wafers and 2 slices of frozen filling. Garnish with a drizzle of balsamic vinegar. Dust with a little Maldon salt and serve immediately with a shot of Kir Royal.
● For the Kir Royal cocktail, pour the Cassis into the bottom of a small grappa glass and top with champagne.

BONBON
OF DUCK LIVER, HAZELNUTS AND NUTELLA WITH PEACHES AND SOFT RECIOTO WINE JELLY

LUISA VALAZZA – AL SORRISO (SORISO, NO)

An unusual sweet-savory appetizer dedicated by Luisa Valazza to the jar that «calms her senses...». «For me, a spoonful of Nutella eaten when you are angry and raging can calm everything down. When I buy a jar, I find it irresistible, I just have to finish it. Then I feel happy and at peace, there's a sense of total satisfaction».

SERVES 4

blanched hazelnuts, IGP Piedmont,		
toasted	2 oz	g 50
peaches	2	
NUTELLA® spread	5 oz	g 150
puff pastry	½ lb	g 200

For the duck liver terrine:

duck liver	10 oz	g 300
dry vermouth	1 T	
cognac	2 T	
granulated sugar	1 T	
dried apricots	6-7	
salt and pepper		

For the wine jelly:

Recioto wine	2 cups	ml 500
gelatin	1 sheet	

To decorate:

peach	1

● Remove the fat from the duck liver, cut into pieces, place in a terrine, and sprinkle with the vermouth and cognac. Season with sugar, salt and pepper, and marinate for 12 hours. After this time, pass the liver through a fine mesh strainer and then spread a rectangle of liver about ⅓" thick on a sheet of aluminum foil. Top with the chopped apricots, then roll it on to itself, pressing the edges together firmly. Steam cook in an oven at 176 °F for 30 minutes, cool immediately in water and ice. Remove the foil and cut the duck liver terrine into four round slices.

● For the wine jelly: heat the Recioto wine and stir in the gelatin, previously softened in cold water. Let cool, then whisk.

● Dice the peaches.

● Place the puff pastry on a work surface. Cut out 4 squares, 3"x3", and bake in a pre-heated 350 °F oven for 8-10 minutes.

● Spread the Nutella on the duck liver terrine slices and sprinkle with the hazelnuts.

● To serve: in the center of each plate place 2 spoonfuls of wine jelly. Using a 2" cookie cutter, place a layer of peach cubes in the jelly, then place a pastry square on top, and cover with a slice of the duck liver terrine. Decorate with thinly sliced peaches.

STRAWBERRY-CHOC

ILARIO VINCIGUERRA – ILARIO VINCIGUERRA RESTAURANT (GALLIATE, VA)

A dessert that's a sheer tingling delight for the taste buds. For Ilario Vinciguerra, Nutella has a particularly seductive side to it: «In 2003 I'd already opened this restaurant and I invited Marika to dinner; she'd been one of my students at a cookery course. I'd fallen in love with her and to try and win her heart I prepared a chocolate cake with a soft Nutella center. Evidently it worked: today Marika is my wife and the manager of our restaurant».

SERVES 4

chocolate crispy	2 oz	g 60
butter	3 cup	g 80
For the ice-cream:		
whole milk	4 cups	l 1
granulated sugar	1 cup	g 200
NUTELLA® spread	1 lb 5 oz	g 600
gelatin		
(softened in cold water		
and squeezed dry)	2 sheets	
eggs	3	
For the caramelized hazelnuts:		
whole blanched hazelnuts,		
toasted	½ lb	g 200
granulated sugar	½ cup	g 100
For the strawberry sauce:		
fresh strawberries	1 lb	g 400
granulated sugar	¾ cup	g 180
mint leaves	5	
For the sponge disc:		
granulated sugar	1 cup	g 250
all-purpose flour	1 cup	g 150
potato flour	3 cup	g 50
baking powder	1 t	
eggs	4	
butter		

As garnish:	
fresh thyme leaves	
sprigs of mint	4
vanilla bean	4

● For the ice-cream: blend all the ingredients together, place in a quick freeze at -4 °F for 3 hours, then whisk with a Pacojet.

● For the caramelized hazelnuts: place the sugar in a small deep-bottomed saucepan, allow to caramelize over a low flame, then add the hazelnuts and while still hot, pour the mixture onto a sheet of parchment paper. Allow to cool completely and, when hard, crush into pieces with a rolling-pin.

● For the sauce: clean the strawberries and dice, sauté with sugar in a pan over a high flame for a few minutes. Scent with the finely chopped mint leaves and allow to cool.

● Prepare the sponge: preheat the oven to 350 °F and lightly butter a 10" cake pan. Using an electric beater, beat the eggs with the sugar until light yellow and creamy. Sift the all-purpose flour, potato flour and baking powder together and gently fold into the egg mixture. Pour into the prepared pan and bake for 25 minutes. Remove the sponge from the cake pan and using two 3" and 1½" pastry cutters cut out 4 donut shapes 2" high. Just before serving, sauté each donut over very low heat in a little butter.

● To serve: place 2 spoonfuls of the very cold strawberry sauce on the bottom of each plate, and top with the hot sponge "donut". Garnish with caramelized hazelnut pieces, the chocolate crispy (Peta Zeta produced by Sosa), and a few thyme leaves. Finally, add a quenelle of ice-cream, decorate with a vanilla bean and a sprig of mint.

PIZZA S'MORE

JONATHAN WAXMAN – BARBUTO (NEW YORK)

A pizza with Nutella inspired by "s'mores", America's iconic treat of campfire roasted marshmallows nestled between chocolate and graham crackers. Here Jonathan Waxman substitutes delicious pizza for the graham crackers for a modern Italian twist on this American classic. Of Nutella he says: «My son Alexander eats it every day for breakfast, and on pizza it's simply fantastic…».

FOR 2 PIZZAS

organic flour	2 cups	g 250
yeast	1 T	g 15
beer	2 T	ml 30
honey	1 T	
extra-virgin olive oil	1 T	
NUTELLA® spread	9 oz	g 250
marshmallows	12	
raspberries	½ lb	g 250

To decorate:
confectioners' sugar
cocoa powder

● Prepare the pizza dough: in a bowl mix the yeast with ½ cup warm water, beer and honey. On a work surface sift the flour into a mound. Create a hollow in the center and slowly pour in the yeast mixture. Mix, using a fork at first and then your hands, until dough forms. Cover with a cloth napkin and let rise for 2 hours.

● Preheat the oven to 500 °F. Divide the dough in half, and roll out each with a rolling pin, until you obtain two round pizzas. Bake separately for 3 minutes.

● Remove from the oven and spread with Nutella.

● Place 6 marshmallows on each pizza and put back in the oven until the marshmallows are completely melted. Remove from oven and top with the raspberries and a dusting of confectioners' sugar and cocoa powder.

● If you like, you can create little mini pizzas, as pictured here. Instead of 2 large pizzas, use a 3 or 4" cookie cutter and cut out small individual portions instead.

DOLCE DOGE

ANDREA ZANIN – PASTICCERIA ZANIN (MESTRE, VENEZIA)

Pastry chef Andrea Zanin dedicates this dessert to his beloved city Venice, which is as varied and intriguing as the many delicious layers of this cake. Andrea Zanin admits: «My whole family loves Nutella. I remember one evening going into the kitchen and checking out the pantry for one last spoonful, only to find that my son had done that old trick of emptying the Nutella jar leaving just a thin layer of chocolate cream on the sides, so the jar still looked full! But how could I tell him off?».

FOR APPROX 30 SMALL PORTIONS

NUTELLA® spread	14 oz	g 400

For the almond sponge:

almond flour	2 cups	g 350
all-purpose flour	¾ cup	g 100
whole eggs	2 cups	g 500
butter, melted	½ cup	g 100
granulated sugar	½ cup	g 100

For the vanilla cream:

confectioners' sugar	1 ¼ cup	g 180
butter, softened	1 cup	g 250
condensed milk	4 T	g 50
vanilla beans	2	
vanilla liqueur	3 T	g 30

Rum syrup for the sponge:

water	1 cup	g 200
granulated sugar	1 cup	g 200
rum (at least 7 years old)	½ cup	g 80

For the glaze:

dark chocolate (70% cocoa)	14 oz	g 400

● Prepare the sponge cake: mix the almond flour, sugar, and eggs and mix well. Sift in the flour and add the butter, mixing until well combined. Place three 8"x12" sheets of parchment paper on a baking tray, pour about 1¼ cup of the mixture onto the sheets and cook in a ventilated oven at 392 °F for 10 minutes.

● For the vanilla cream: mix the butter and confectioners' sugar and whisk until light yellow, then add the condensed milk, vanilla, and vanilla liqueur and mix well.

● For the syrup: bring the water and sugar to a boil. Remove from the heat and add the rum.

● On a parchment-lined work surface place a layer of sponge, moisten it with the rum syrup, and then spread a layer of vanilla cream on top.

● Top with another sponge layer, moisten with the rum syrup and spread with (¾ cup) of Nutella. Cover with the last layer of sponge. Mix the remaining Nutella into the remaining vanilla cream and spread over the sponge cake. Let cool. Cut into rectangles, 2"x1", and glaze with 1½ cups of dark chocolate melted at 104 °F.

● Garnish each slice, if you like.

CREAMY RISOTTO
WITH PUMPKIN AND NUTELLA

LUCA ZECCHIN – RELAIS SAN MAURIZIO, RISTORANTE GUIDO DA COSTIGLIOLE (SANTO STEFANO BELBO, CN)

An unusual and incredibly delicious first course! You'll be amazed at how well Nutella pairs with pumpkin. Luca confesses: «Nutella was part of family life, a memory of my childhood breakfasts. Sometimes, even now, before going to sleep after a long day's work... I look for Nutella».

SERVES 4

Carnaroli rice	1 ½ cups	g 400
pumpkin, cleaned and cubed	½ lb	g 200
butter	₃ cup	g 100
Parmigiano cheese, grated	₃ cup	g 70
Moscato d'Asti wine	₃ cup	cl 10
onion, chopped	½ oz	g 15
shallot, chopped	1	
NUTELLA® spread	2 T	g 40

● Sauté the onion in a little butter until translucent, and then add the pumpkin. Stir and cook until the pumpkin is lightly browned, then add a ladleful of water and cook, covered, over very low heat. When the pumpkin starts to fall apart, remove from the heat, and purée in a blender or food processor and reserve.

● In a saucepan sauté the shallot until translucent, then add the rice and stir for 3-4 minutes. Add the Moscato wine and stir until evaporated. Add 2 ladlefuls of hot water, and continue cooking, stirring with a wooden spoon, and adding more hot water as the rice dries out. Towards the end of the cooking time stir in the reserved pumpkin purée until well blended and then stir in the butter and Parmigiano cheese. The mixture should have a creamy consistency.

● Pour the rice onto individual serving plates and top with a teaspoon of Nutella. Serve immediately.

THE SCENT OF HOME

Home cooking, food prepared and served with love. Everything from recipes to wake up the whole family at breakfast to simple cookies for children's parties, tea-time treats, puddings and cakes. All with one extra ingredient, Nutella, which adds a touch of delight and passion. Recipes from my childhood, carefully guarded in my mother Olga's faded cookbook, as well as recipes from dear friends, like my English friend who shared her recipe for Chelsea buns, and said, «Happiness is a Chelsea bun. When you share it with someone it's like a pic-nic. A recipe that isn't shared will be forgotten, while a recipe that is shared will be enjoyed by future generations».

FOR BREAKFAST

MARBLE YOGURT RING CAKE

SERVES 6

plain European-style yogurt	½ cup	g 125
granulated sugar	¾ cup	g 200
all-purpose flour	1 ¾ cups	g 210
corn oil	½ cup	g 100
NUTELLA® spread	⅓ cup	g 85
eggs	3	
salt	a pinch	
lemon zest	1	
baking powder	1 T	
confectioners' sugar		

In Italy, this sort of cake can be either sweet or savory. The important thing is that it has a hole in the middle! In this sweet version, Nutella is marbled with the lighter cake batter to create a pleasing visual effect.

In a large mixing bowl, beat the eggs together with the sugar using a hand-held electric beater or a whisk. Slowly sift in the flour, baking powder, and a pinch of salt. Continue whisking, then add the yogurt, corn oil and lemon zest. ● Preheat the oven to 350 °F and lightly butter and flour a 10" ring mold or Bundt pan. Pour half of the mixture into the pan. Blend the Nutella into the remaining batter until well combined, then swirl it into the batter in the pan. ● Bake for about 30 minutes, until a toothpick inserted into the center comes out clean. Cool, turn out onto a serving platter, and dust with confectioners' sugar.

MUESLI AND CHOCOLATE CHIP MUFFINS

MAKES 6 MUFFINS

plain yogurt	½ cup	g 100
NUTELLA® spread	¼ cup	g 60
all-purpose flour	½ cup	g 50
crunchy muesli or oat flakes	1 oz	g 30
corn flour	1 ½ T	g 20
granulated sugar	2 ½ T	g 30
butter, softened	2 T	g 30
egg	1	
milk	1 t	
baking powder	1 t	g 4
dark chocolate chips	3 T	g 30

A variation on the classic American muffin, ideal for breakfast and great for an afternoon snack. Studded with chocolate chips, they are even special enough for dessert!

In a large mixing bowl combine the flour, corn flour, muesli and baking powder. ● In a bowl, beat the eggs with an electric hand-held beater and slowly beat in the sugar, butter, yogurt and milk until blended. Add the flour mixture, a little at a time, and mix carefully. ● Add the Nutella and 2 tablespoons of the chocolate chips. Do not overmix or the muffins will not be light. Let rest for 15 minutes. ● Butter silicone muffin molds or a muffin tray. Preheat the oven to 335 °F. Fill each mold a little more than halfway with batter and sprinkle with the remaining chocolate chips. Bake for 25 minutes. ● Remove from the oven and let cool for at least 5-10 minutes before unmolding. Serve warm.

Nutella passion | For Breakfast

SPICY BREAD

SERVES 8

egg whites	4	
granulated sugar	½ cup	g 120
all-purpose flour	1 cup	g 110
NUTELLA® spread	½ cup	g 100
chestnut flour	¼ cup	g 50
butter, softened	3 T	g 40
ground cinnamon	½ t	
ground nutmeg	½ t	
ground star anise	½ t	

A surprisingly delicious bread that comes together quickly with just a few simple ingredients. Makes a nutritious breakfast or tasty snack. Add it to lunch boxes for a healthy treat. Wrapped in foil it keeps nicely for several days.

Place the egg whites in a large bowl and whisk for a few seconds, until just mixed. Slowly mix in the sugar and then sift in the all-purpose and chestnut flours. ● Stir the mixture for a few minutes and then add the Nutella, a teaspoon at a time. ● Finally, add the softened butter. Vigorously beat the mixture for 10 minutes and then add the spices. ● Preheat the oven to 325 °F and butter a rectangular baking pan (about 10"x15"). Pour the batter into the prepared pan and bake for 35-40 minutes. ● Remove from the oven and serve cold or warm, cut into thick squares. ● Note: you can substitute an equal amount of potato or all-purpose flour for the chestnut flour, if you prefer.

CHELSEA BUNS

SERVES 6

all-purpose flour	2 ½ cups	g 300
raisins	4 oz	g 120
whole milk	½ cup	ml 120
NUTELLA® spread	¼ cup	g 60
granulated sugar	¼ cup	g 50
butter, softened	2 T	g 30
egg	1	
active dry yeast	⅓ oz	g 10
salt	a pinch	

These small snail-shaped bread rolls originated in the famous Chelsea Bun House in London in the 18th century. It is said that King George II was extremely fond of them. Unfortunately the Bun House closed down in 1839, but luckily the recipe has survived. Adding Nutella gives the buns a really special "swirl".

Soak the raisins in a small bowl with a little warm water until softened, then drain, pat dry and reserve. ● Sift the flour and the salt and divide between two mixing bowls. ● In a small saucepan, heat the milk until just warmed; remove from heat, sprinkle on the yeast and let rest to activate. Remember that the milk shouldn't be too hot otherwise the yeast won't activate. ● Slowly pour the milk-yeast mixture into one of the bowls of flour and mix well. ● To the other bowl beat in the sugar, softened butter and lightly whisked egg. ● Now add the yeast-flour to the mixture and knead for 10 minutes, until smooth. Cover the bowl with a cloth, and let rise in a warm place for one hour. ● Preheat the oven to to 400 °F. Roll out the dough on a lightly floured work surface into a rectangle, ¼" thick. Using a spatula spread with a thin layer of Nutella and evenly sprinkle with the reserved raisins. Carefully roll the dough lengthwise. Using a sharp knife cut slices approximately ¾" thick. ● Place the slices, very close together forming a large circle, onto a baking pan. Bake for about 15 minutes. Serve warm.

ORANGE "PLUM" CAKE

SERVES 6

all-purpose flour	1 cup	g 135
raisins	4 oz	g 100
candied orange peel, diced	3 oz	g 80
butter, softened	5 T	g 70
heavy cream	¼ cup	ml 60
granulated sugar	¼ cup	g 50
NUTELLA® spread	3 T	g 60
large eggs	3	
baking powder	2 t	g 10
vanilla extract	1 t	
orange	1 ½	
orange oil or extract	1 t	ml 4

Pellegrino Artusi, in his 19th-century treatise *Science in the Kitchen and the Art of Eating Well*, lists this cake recipe alongside a "plum pudding" recipe. Both desserts are of English origin and neither contains plums. Therefore, the great gastronomist of Forlimpopoli describes plum cake as «lying to itself about its own name». However, what Artusi did not realize is that the term comes from the fact that in England in the past both currants and raisins were often called "plums," and were ingredients found in both plum pudding and plum cake. This version of the English classic has a Mediterranean twist – a hint of orange and a touch of Nutella, a winning combination. If you like, substitute an equal weight of almonds, pine nuts, walnuts or pistachios for the candied orange peel.

Grate the orange reserving the zest, and then squeeze the juice from half of the orange. Pour the juice into a bowl, add the raisins and let soften for at least 20 minutes, stirring occasionally. ● Meanwhile, in a mixing bowl, beat the butter with a wooden spoon or an electric hand-held mixer, until light yellow and creamy. Beat in the sugar until blended. Add the eggs, one by one, and sift in the flour and baking powder. Add the vanilla extract and stir until combined. ● In a separate bowl, whip the cream until it doubles in volume but remains soft; slowly incorporate the Nutella, a teaspoon at a time. Blend delicately, from the bottom of the bowl to the top so that the whipped cream remains firm. ● Add spoonfuls of this mixture to the batter, then add the raisins, candied orange peel and orange oil and mix until combined. ● Butter and flour a loaf pan (about 10x26 cm, 4"x10"). Preheat the oven to 350 °F. Pour the batter into the prepared pan and bake for about 45 minutes until a toothpick inserted in the center comes out clean. ● Serve warm or at room temperature.

COOKIES

LEMON SHORTBREAD COOKIES

MAKES ABOUT 30 COOKIES

all-purpose flour	2 ¼ cups	g 280
sugar	⅓ cup	g 95
corn oil	⅓ cup	g 75
NUTELLA® spread	2 T	g 40
egg	1	
egg yolk	1	
salt	a pinch	
lemon zest	1	
lemon juice	1 T	

For the glaze:

egg whites	2	
confectioners' sugar	1 ¼ cups	g 175
lemon juice	1 T	

These simple-to-make, homey cookies, evoke childhood memories of mornings spent with the family in a warm kitchen filled with the scent of freshly brewed coffee and sipping steaming mugs of hot milk. I've updated a medieval recipe to include Nutella, and have substituted oil for the butter for a lighter cookie.

On a clean, smooth surface or in a large mixing bowl, sift the flour and make a hollow in the center; pour the oil and salt into the hallow. Mix with a fork, slowly incorporating the ingredients until it resembles coarse sand. ● Make a hollow in the center again and add the eggs, sugar, lemon zest and juice. Mix together quickly until just combined then add the Nutella and knead briefly just until dough forms. ● Roll the dough into a ball and refrigerate for at least 1 hour. Then place the dough on a floured surface and roll it out with a lightly floured rolling pin to a thickness of ¼". Use any shape cookie cutter – stars, hearts, or flowers – and cut out the cookies. ● Pre-heat the oven to 350 °F. Place the cookies, leaving space between each, onto a parchment lined baking pan, and bake for 20 minutes. Let cool. ● If you like, you can glaze the cookies. To make the glaze whisk together the egg whites, confectioners' sugar and lemon juice until smooth. Spread on the cooled cookies.

MELIGA COOKIES

MAKES ABOUT 40 COOKIES

corn flour	1 cup	g 130
all-purpose flour	1 cup	g 110
butter, softened and diced	½ cup	g 130
confectioners' sugar	½ cup	g 80
NUTELLA® spread	⅓ cup	g 80
egg yolks	2	
salt	a pinch	

These cookies, made with wholesome corn flour, are a traditional Piedmont treat, and in fact, their name comes from the local dialect for corn flour. The corn flour adds a lovely crunch while the Nutella adds rich flavor. Meliga cookies are wonderful for dessert, served with zabaglione and a small glass of sweet Moscato wine.

Sift the two flours into a mixing bowl, then add the confectioners' sugar and salt. Mix well. Add the butter and the egg yolks, one at a time; and finally the Nutella. ● Work the ingredients together quickly until you obtain a smooth, blended dough. Roll sections of the dough into finger-width sticks about 5" to 6" long. Shape them any way you like – in rings, half-moons, or "S"s. ● Lightly butter and flour a baking sheet and preheat the oven to 400 °F. Place the cookies on the prepared baking sheet and bake for about 10 minutes, until just lightly golden. ● Allow to cool completely before removing them with a spatula onto a serving platter.

Nutella passion | Cookies

SUNDAY COOKIES WITH HOT CHOCOLATE

MAKES ABOUT 35 COOKIES

For the cookies:

all-purpose flour	1 cup	g 110
granulated sugar	½ cup	g 100
potato flour	½ cup	g 80
eggs	2	
ground star anise	1 t	
ground cinnamon	1 t	
ground ginger	1 t	

For 4 cups of hot chocolate:

NUTELLA® spread	1 cup	g 240
whole milk	1 cup	ml 250

«Sunday pastries», according to the French writer Philippe Delerm, «should be carried home dangling from the bow that ties the package, like a pendulum». Among the many long-lost memories of the past, to recall with nostalgia, are these little cookies which in my childhood were made at home. The ritual had three specific moments: the batter was made on a Saturday evening, baked the next morning before going to church, and then eaten upon our return, along with delicious hot chocolate, a treat we eagerly waited for all week. I offer you the recipe and have added Nutella.

In a large mixing bowl whisk the eggs until frothy. Add the sugar and continue to whisk until dense and creamy. ● Sift in the all-purpose flour, potato flour and spices, and gently, using a spoon so as not to flatten the whisked eggs, fold the mixture until combined. ● Line two baking pans with parchment paper. Using 2 spoons, place small coin-shaped dollops of the mixture on the pans, leaving space between the cookies. Let rest overnight in a warm place. ● The next morning, bake the cookies for 20-25 minutes. Eat them with hot chocolate. ● To make the hot chocolate: put the Nutella in a heavy-bottomed saucepan and slowly add the milk, stirring with a wooden spoon. Place the saucepan over a very low heat and stir continuously for a few minutes, until it thickens slightly and coats the spoon. Serve hot or warm.

Nutella passion | The Scent of Home

ZALETI MORI

MAKES 20 COOKIES

fine corn flour	½ cup	g 60
all-purpose flour	½ cup	g 60
sugar	1 ½ oz	g 40
butter, melted	2 T	g 30
NUTELLA® spread	2 T	g 30
raisins	1 ¼ oz	g 35
egg	1	
baking powder	½ t	
salt	a pinch	
pine nuts, optional	1 oz	g 30
confectioners' sugar		

«Dear Mothers, treat your children to these little cakes, but beware not to taste them yourselves, unless you want your little ones to cry because there will be less for them to eat», jokes Pellegrino Artusi about these Venetian cookies in his 1891 book *Science in the Kitchen and the Art of Eating Well*. Their name comes from the Venetian dialect for yellow, the color of the corn flour. I've prepared them adding Nutella: the result is delicious.

Soak the raisins in warm water or sweet white wine for at least 30 minutes. Drain and dry with a paper towel. ● Mix the flours, salt, and baking powder; add the melted butter and knead. ● In a mixing bowl, using an electric hand-held mixer, beat the egg and sugar until light yellow and creamy. Slowly, a little at a time, incorporate it into the flour mixture. ● Add the raisins, pine nuts, if using, and Nutella. Mix all the ingredients. Make two rolls from the dough 1½" in diameter and cut into 2½" lengths. Mold them into diamond-like shapes with rounded edges approx ¼" thick. ● Line a baking pan with parchment paper and preheat the oven to 325-335 °F. Put them 1" apart onto the prepared pan and bake for 15 minutes. ● Remove from the oven and dust with confectioners' sugar before they cool. They keep for several days in an air-tight container.

Nutella passion | Cookies

LINGUE DI GATTO (CAT TONGUE COOKIES)

MAKES ABOUT 35 COOKIES

all-purpose flour	¾ cup	g 100
butter	4 T	g 60
confectioners' sugar	⅓ cup	g 60
NUTELLA® spread	¼ cup	g 70
egg whites	2	

These are small cookies, are very light and have a delicate taste. They get their name from their distinctive shape and from the "roughness" of the texture. In this version, the addition of Nutella imparts a lovely dark golden color and the wonderfully warm aroma of hazelnuts. Delicious alone, and unforgettable when paired with ice-cream or pudding!

Soften the butter for 2 hours at room temperature, then beat with a wooden spoon until creamy. Sift in the confectioners' sugar and beat until the mixture is creamy. Gently fold in the Nutella. ● In another bowl, using a whisk, lightly beat the egg whites for a few seconds; they should not be stiff. Add them a spoonful at a time to the butter mixture. Finally slowly sift in the flour. Do not over-beat or the cookies will be tough. ● Line a baking pan with parchment paper and preheat the oven to 335 °F. Put the batter into a pastry bag with a smooth opening, and press out the mixture, directly onto the pan, in sticks approx 2″ long, and about 2″ apart. They will spread during baking. ● Bake for about 8 minutes, until all the edges are crisp but the centers are still soft. ● Remove from the oven and cool on a baking rack. The cookies will stay fragrant for several days.

Nutella passion | The Scent of Home

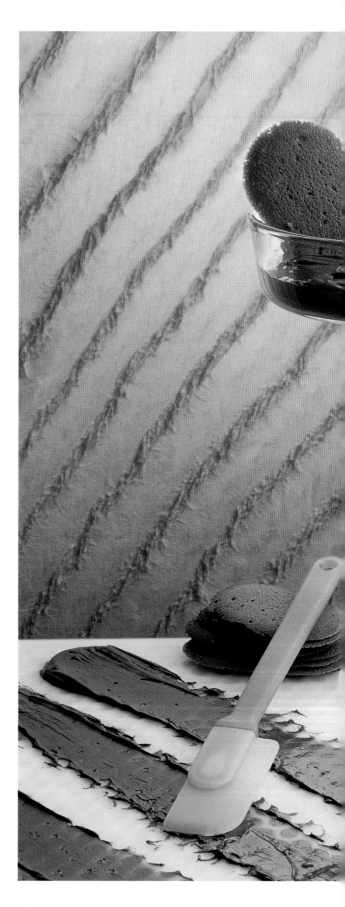

CANTUCCI

MAKES 24 CANTUCCI

all-purpose flour	1 ½ cups	g 170
butter	2 T	g 30
granulated sugar	¼ cup	g 50
blanched almonds, chopped	2 ½ oz	g 70
NUTELLA® spread	2 T	g 30
egg	1	
egg yolk	1	
baking powder	1 t	g 5-6
lemon zest	½	
orange zest	½	
salt	a pinch	

Cantucci, also called "Biscuits of Prato", are made in nearly every bakery or pastry shop in Tuscany. They are usually enjoyed dipped into Vin Santo or other dessert wines. My recipe adds a touch of color and taste with Nutella.

Slightly melt the butter in a bain-marie and reserve. ● On a work surface (or in a large mixing bowl) place the flour in a mound and add the sugar, egg, salt, baking powder and zests. ● Mix well, then slowly add the Nutella, a little at a time, and finally the reserved butter and almonds. ● Knead the dough for a few minutes, then divide it into two small loaves about 12" long and 2" wide. Line a baking pan with parchment paper and preheat the oven to 350 °F. Place the loaves, separated by several inches, onto the prepared pan and carefully brush with the beaten egg yolk. Bake for 20 minutes. ● Remove the loaves from the oven and while still hot cut them on an angle into slices about ½" thick. Put the cantucci back into the oven for 5 minutes, until firm. Cool on a baking rack.

Nutella passion | Cookies

TEGOLE (ROOF TILES)

MAKES 40 COOKIES

granulated sugar	⅓ cup	g 80
hazelnuts, toasted	2 ½ oz	g 65
blanched almonds	2 ½ oz	g 65
bitter almonds, optional	2-3	
butter, melted	2 ½ T	g 35
eggs, separated	2	
all-purpose flour	¼ cup	g 25
NUTELLA® spread	2 T	g 30
salt	a pinch	

Thin delicate cookies prepared with finely ground almonds and hazelnuts. It is said that the recipe was kept secret for many years. Their name comes from the fact that they are left to dry on a rolling pin or any other cylindrical object so they take on a shape reminiscent of the roof tiles on the houses in the Val d'Aosta region of Italy. A traditional variation glazes them with dark chocolate; instead we propose this version with Nutella which give you tiles of an intense nut-brown color.

Lightly butter a baking pan and preheat the oven to 340 °F (a convection oven is best). Combine the almonds and the hazelnuts in a food processor and grind them until they resemble fine sand. Reserve. ● Put the egg yolks and the sugar in a mixing bowl, and with an electric hand-held beater beat until frothy. Using a spoon slowly stir in all but ¼ cup of the reserved nuts, butter, flour, and Nutella. ● Mix until well combined. In a separate bowl, whisk the egg whites and salt until stiff peaks form and fold into the batter. ● Drop rounded spoonfuls of the batter, about 2″-2½″ in diameter, onto the baking sheet, leaving plenty of space between the cookies. Sprinkle with the reserved ¼ cup of hazelnuts and bake for 15 minutes until only the edges are golden. Remove them from the oven and, while still soft and hot, using a spatula lay them carefully on a rolling pin or the side of a bottle so they take on their distinctive roof tile shape. ● Remember that, although they'll still be delicious, if you let them cool down they'll become crisp and fragile and it won't be possible to curve them.

The Scent of Home | Nutella passion

WITH TEA

BRUTTI E BUONI (UGLY BUT GOOD)

MAKES ABOUT 20 COOKIES

toasted hazelnuts	3 ½ oz	g 100
granulated sugar	⅓ cup	g 80
egg whites	2	g 70
NUTELLA® spread	2 T	g 40
salt	a pinch	
ground cinnamon	½ t	

It is their rather rustic appearance and irregular shape that gives these cookies their distinctive name. In this Nutella version they are still "ugly", though they are much better than just "good". They can also be made with almonds, if you like. Theses classic cookies from northern Italy stay crunchy and keep for a long time when stored in an air-tight container.

Coarsely chop half the hazelnuts and finely crush the remaining half with a knife or a rolling pin. ● In a mixing bowl whisk the egg whites and salt until stiff peaks form. Folding delicately from the bottom to the top, blend in the sugar, cinnamon, chopped and crushed hazelnuts. Next, slowly drizzle in the Nutella, being careful not to deflate the mixture. ● Pour into a heavy-bottomed wide saucepan and over very low heat, stirring continuously with a wooden spoon, simmer for about 10 minutes, until thick, shiny, and slightly sticky. ● Preheat the oven to 280-300 °F and line two baking pans with either aluminum foil or parchment paper. Place irregular spoonfuls of the mixture, leaving space between them, onto the prepared pans and bake for 20-25 minutes until they are dry and meringue-like. ● Store in an air-tight container and the *brutti e buoni* can be kept for many days without losing their fragrance.

BACI DI DAMA (LADY'S KISSES)

MAKES 25-30 COOKIES

all-purpose flour	¾ cup	g 100
sugar	½ cup	g 100
butter, diced	7 T	g 100
blanched almonds	4 ½ oz	g 100
bitter almonds, optional	2-3	
NUTELLA® spread	3 T	g 60

These traditional cookies from Piedmont, charmingly called "lady's kisses", are two almondy cookie spheres usally held together with dark chocolate. In this version, they are connected with a delicious dollop of Nutella.

Preheat the oven to 350 °F. Spread the almonds onto a baking pan and bake until just golden. Let cool and then combine them with the sugar in a food processor and grind until fine. ● Put the almonds into a mixing bowl, sift in the flour and add the butter. Using your finger tips quickly mix together until just blended, form a ball, cover with plastic wrap, and refrigerate for 45 minutes. ● Using your hands, roll out sections about ½" in diameter. Cut into ½" segments and roll into small balls. Place on a parchment lined baking pan, leaving space between each cookie. Bake for 15-20 minutes, until golden. ● Let cool to room temperature and then join the two half spheres together with a teaspoon of Nutella. ● Let rest a few hours so the halves properly adhere, and serve.

Nutella passion | With Tea

MACAROONS

MAKES 25-30 MACAROONS

For the macaroons:

blanched almonds	4 oz	g 125
granulated sugar	1 cup	g 225
egg whites	3	g 100
confectioners' sugar	⅓ cup	g 50

For the filling:

whipped cream	½ cup	g 100
NUTELLA® spread	3 T	g 50

Today Paris would not be Paris without the chance to taste and compare its many varieties of macaroons, from those made by acclaimed pastry chef and chocolate-maker Pierre Hermé, to the classic version of Ladurée, two shops in the Latin Quarter, just a stone's throw from each other. The following macaroons are an easy homemade version with a Nutella filling: sweet and irresistible.

Preheat the oven to 335 °F and line a baking sheet with parchment paper. Put the almonds and ½ cup of the granulated sugar in a food processor and grind until fine. Transfer to a bowl and combine with the confectioners' sugar. ● In a separate bowl whisk the egg whites until stiff peaks form, then slowly add the remaining ½ cup of granulated sugar and then quickly fold in the almond mixture. ● Place the meringue mixture into a pastry bag with a smooth tip attachment and squeeze out evenly spaced small spheres of the mixture which, while cooking, will expand to 2"-2¼". Let rest for 30 minutes, then bake for 12 minutes. ● Make the filling: put the whipped cream into a bowl and carefully fold in the Nutella, taking care not to deflate the mixture. ● Allow the macaroons to cool, then connect two halves with the Nutella filling. ● If you can restrain yourselves the macaroons taste even better the next day! The unfilled macaroons can be kept in an air-tight tin for 2-3 days.

COCONUTS

MAKES ABOUT 30 COOKIES

grated coconut	4 oz	g 100
plus more for garnish		
granulated sugar	⅓ cup	g 80
NUTELLA® spread	4 T	g 75
egg whites	2	
salt	a pinch	

Coconut has been one of the most widely-used "exotic" ingredients in pastry-making since the beginning of the last century. In the various attempts to perfect the recipe, found beautifully handwritten in my mother's pastry notebook, these delicious cookies have always been universally approved by the "tasters". There's only one problem: if you try one, you'll have a hard time not eating the rest!

Pre-heat the oven to 350 °F and line a baking pan with aluminum foil or parchment paper. Place the egg whites and salt in a mixing bowl and beat lightly with a fork until just combined, but absolutely not frothy. ● Using a spoon, stir in the sugar and coconut, until just blended, then carefully add the Nutella. The mixture must be well blended but not liquidy. ● Using a teaspoon, take small amounts of the mixture and, using your hands, make small balls and place on the baking pan. ● Bake for 10-15 minutes. Garnish with a sprinkling of finely-ground coconut.

Nutella passion | With Tea

MADELEINES

MAKES ABOUT 12

all-purpose flour	⅞ cup	g 100
butter	4 T	g 60
granulated sugar	¼ cup	g 60
NUTELLA® spread	1 T	g 20
eggs	2	
baking powder	2 pinches	
confectioners' sugar	1 heaping T	
orange blossom water	1 t	
lemon zest	½	
salt	a pinch	

Tradition has it that these little Parisian cakes were invented by a certain Madeleine, a servant to the king of Poland who had em-igrated to France in 1760. They're soft and fragrant, to be enjoyed with a cup of tea or coffee. They certainly could not have been left out of this collection of recipes, since many people associate the adult passion for Nutella with the classic "Proustian madeleine" – according to the meaning given in Proust's *À la recherche du temps perdu* – as a memory of the tastes of childhood. I wonder what Aunt Léonie would have thought about it?

Butter 12 shell-shaped madeleine molds, preferably silicone, and preheat the oven to 375 °F. Sift the flour with the baking powder and reserve. Melt the butter over a very low flame or bain-marie; making sure it does not begin to color. Remove from the heat and stir in the Nutella until fully blended. ● Com-bine the eggs, sugar and salt, and using either an electric hand-held beater or standing mixer beat the mixture for a long time (Pellegrino Artusi suggests at least 15 minutes in his recipe for "madeleine dough"), until it has quadrupled and is opaque. ● Slowly add the flour and baking powder, dusting it on through a fine mesh strainer, and fold in with a metal spoon, making circular movements from top to bottom. Fold in the zest, drizzle in the butter-Nutella mixture, and orange blossom water. I found the reminder hand-written in my mother's cook book: «At the end, don't forget the orange blossom water». ● Pour the mixture into each mold up to ¾ full and bake for 15 minutes until they rise and are golden. ● Remove from the oven and using a thin knife tip, pop them out of the molds and onto a wire rack. Serve dusted with confectioners' sugar.

Nutella passion | The Scent of Home

RICCIARELLI

MAKES 50 SMALL COOKIES

blanched almonds, lightly toasted	10 oz	g 300
granulated sugar	1 ¼ cups	g 300
confectioners' sugar	¼ cup	g 30
NUTELLA® spread	¼ cup	g 65
egg whites	2	
vanilla extract	a few drops	
lemon zest	½	
orange blossom water	1 t	ml 5
salt	a pinch	

These are typical cookies from Siena and other Tuscan provinces. Soft, very sweet, and with a wrinkled and cracked surface, they are direct descendants of classic marzipan. My *ricciarelli* with Nutella are darker than the very pale originals.

Line a baking pan with parchment paper and preheat the oven to 325 °F. ● Finely grind the almonds and sugar in a food processor. Transfer to a mixing bowl and add the lemon zest, vanilla, orange blossom water and Nutella spread, a little at a time. Blend until well combined. ● Whisk the egg whites and salt until stiff peaks form and slowly fold into the almond mixture. Stir with a wooden spoon until dense enough to be worked with your hands, like dough. ● Generously dust a work surface with confectioners' sugar and roll out the dough to a 1" thickness. Using a knife dipped in confectioners' sugar, cut the dough into diamond shapes, about 1 ½"x 2" long. Using a sugar-dusted palette carefully place the *ricciarelli* on the prepared pan, leaving plenty of space between each. ● Bake for about 20 minutes until dry to the touch, but still soft. They should not color at all. ● Let cool and serve, dusted with confectioners' sugar.

SCONES

MAKES 8

all-purpose flour	¾ cup	g 100
NUTELLA® spread	2 T	g 30
granulated sugar	2 T	g 25
butter, diced	2 T	g 25
egg yolk	1	
milk	1 t	ml 5
baking powder	½ t	g 2
salt	a pinch	

Scones, the classic English biscuits, are generally served with strawberry jam and clotted cream or butter. Although there are many recipes for scones, this Nutella version has a distinctive nutty chocolate flavor, which pairs especially wonderfully with jam. If you are in need of a little extra pampering, spread them with Nutella instead!

Sift the flour and baking powder into a bowl and stir in the sugar and salt. Using your fingers, blend in the butter until the mixture resembles coarse sand. Add the milk and Nutella, and mix with a wooden spoon until smooth. Do not overwork the dough or the scones will not be tender. ● Form the dough into a ball, cover with plastic wrap, and refrigerate for about 1 hour. ● Pre-heat the oven to 400 °F. Lightly butter a baking pan. Meanwhile roll the scone dough out on a floured work-surface about ½" thick. Cut out 2" to 2¼" circles using a cookie cutter and place on the prepared baking pan. ● Beat the egg yolk with two tablespoons of water and brush over the scones. Bake for about 18 minutes. ● Serve the scones while still warm (some like to serve them hot).

Nutella passion | With Tea

APRICOT THUMBPRINT COOKIES

MAKES ABOUT 40 COOKIES

blanched almonds, toasted	4 oz	g 100
all-purpose flour	¾ cup	g 100
butter, softened	4 ½ T	g 65
sugar	¼ cup	g 50
NUTELLA® spread	3 T	g 50
apricot jam	8 oz	g 200

Nutella adds a wonderful moistness and flavor to these easy-to-make cookies. I fill them with my own homemade apricot jam, which I love to make every summer, but they are delicious with other flavor jams too.

Line a baking pan with parchment paper and preheat the oven to 350 °F. Grind the almonds in a food processor until they resemble fine sand and reserve. ● In a mixing bowl beat the butter with a wooden spoon until smooth and creamy. Add the sugar, flour, and reserved almonds and mix until well combined. Swirl in the Nutella, but do not mix thoroughly if you want to achieve a marbled effect. ● Roll teaspoonfuls of the mixture in your hands to form small balls and, with your thumb, create a little indent in the center. Place, well spaced, onto the prepared baking pan, and bake for 15-20 minutes. ● After removing from the oven, spoon a little apricot jam into the center of each cookie, allow to cool for a few hours, then serve. ● They will be delicious and soft for several days.

Nutella passion | The Scent of Home

"RICE CAKES"

SERVES 12

butter and breadcrumbs, for the pan		
whole milk	3 ¼ cups	ml 800
long grain white rice	½ cup	g 130
salt	a pinch	
orange zest	½	
granulated sugar	2 T	g 25
candied orange peel, minced	1 oz	g 35
NUTELLA® spread	2 ¾ T	g 50
rum	2 T	
orange marmalade	1 ½ oz	g 40
eggs, separated	3	
ground cinnamon	a pinch	

Cake made with rice is an Italian regional classic, especially in Bologna, where they are baked to celebrate the Feast of the *Addobbi* following *Corpus Domini*. To enjoy these cakes at their best, Pellegrino Artusi (who inspired this recipe) suggests: «They are better eaten when warm rather than cold». Rice is particularly wonderful with Nutella spread.

Preheat the oven to 325 °F and generously butter 12 molds, either "brioche" (as indicated by Artusi) or muffin-sized, or a ring mold or Bundt pan, and dust with breadcrumbs. ● Bring the milk to the boil in a large saucepan; add the rice, salt and orange zest. Do as Artusi suggests: «cook the rice for a long time, stirring frequently so it does not stick». ● Two thirds of the way through the cooking time add the sugar and candied orange. Keep stirring over a moderate flame until all the milk has been absorbed and the rice is soft and well cooked. ● Remove from the heat and allow to cool a little and then add the Nutella, rum, orange marmalade and cinnamon and stir until well combined. Finally, one at a time, add the egg yolks. ● In a mixing bowl whisk the egg whites until stiff. Carefully fold them into the rice mixture. ● Spoon the mixture into the molds until two-thirds full. Bake for about 40 minutes, until golden.

Nutella passion | With Tea

GRANDMOTHER CATERINA'S AMARETTO COOKIES

MAKES ABOUT 80 COOKIES

all-purpose flour	⅔ cup	g 75
fine yellow corn meal	⅓ cup	g 45
blanched hazelnuts, toasted and minced	½ cup	g 85
whole hazelnuts as garnish	3 oz	g 80
butter, softened	4 T	g 50
sugar	¼ cup	g 50
egg yolk	1	
NUTELLA® spread	½ cup	g 100
ground cinnamon	1 t	
rum or amaretto liqueur	1 t	ml 5
confectioners' sugar, optional		

Cookies, pastries and biscuits: the number of different recipes is endless. Each region of Italy, for every festival throughout the year, has a traditional recipe to pass on to future generations. Specialties like amaretto cookies are found in various areas of Italy: each cook has his or her own recipe, like this one belonging to my grandmother Caterina. Since the Langhe area in southern Piedmont is rich in hazelnuts, our family always called these cookies "amaretti", even though they were not made with almonds. I remember my grandmother preparing the dough; I used to like taking little spoonfuls of it, and with my hands make up the balls to place on the baking tray. Then, the final touch: placing a whole hazelnut in the center, a beautiful round one, the ones harvested at the end of summer.

Preheat the oven to 285 °F and line a baking pan with parchment paper. ● Using a hand-held electric mixer, beat the yolk with the sugar until thick and light yellow. Sift in the flours, a spoonful at a time, and then fold in the hazelnuts. Add the butter and slowly, a little at a time, fold in the Nutella, cinnamon, and rum or amaretto liqueur. ● Knead the dough with your hands until all the ingredients are completely blended. With a teaspoon take a small quantity and, rolling with your hands, make small walnut-sized balls with all the dough. Put each ball onto the prepared pan and top with a whole hazelnut. ● Bake for 20 minutes, let cool, and serve dusted with confectioners' sugar if preferred.

Nutella passion | The Scent of Home

PUDDINGS

SOFT-CENTERED CHOCOLATE CAKE

SERVES 6

dark chocolate (60-70% cocoa), chopped	4 oz	g 100
all-purpose flour	⅔ cup	g 80
NUTELLA® spread	¼ cup	g 70
butter, softened	5 T	g 70
sugar	¼ cup	g 50
eggs	2	
baking powder	1 t	g 3
salt	a pinch	

On the menu of many restaurants you'll find "lava cakes", delicious little soft-centered cakes with a small bubble of dark chocolate that oozes out when you plunge your spoon into the center. In this recipe Nutella gives the cake a particular moistness and transforms it into a rich treat.

Lightly butter 6 individual ramekins or silicone molds and preheat the oven to 335 °F. ● Stir the butter in a bowl with a wooden spoon until creamy. Slowly fold in the Nutella, then add the eggs, sugar, and salt. Sift the flour and baking powder. ● Spoon two heaping tablespoons of the batter into each mold and bake for 7 minutes. ● Remove from oven and sprinkle each with dark chocolate. Cover with the remaining batter and return to the oven (still at 335 °F) for 15 minutes. Serve warm.

GIANDUJA CHOCOLATE PUDDING

SERVES 8 PORTIONS

For the caramel:

sugar	¼ cup	g 50
water	2 T	
lemon juice	a few drops	

For the pudding:

milk, warmed	2 cups	l 1½
eggs	4	
granulated sugar	⅓ cup	g 90
NUTELLA® spread	½ cup	g 100
amaretti cookies	2 ½ oz	g 70
hazelnuts, toasted	2 ½ oz	g 70
unsweetened cocoa powder	2 t	g 10
rum	2 T	ml 20
coffee	½ cup	ml 100

The famous *gianduiotto* hazelnut chocolate was created in 1865 by Isidore Caffarel and Michele Prochet, and was named after Gianduja, Turin's carnival character. I have wanted to show you an original version of this traditional Piedmontese pudding that is called *bônet*, which means hat, and refers to its shape after baking.

Prepare the caramel: place the sugar, water and lemon juice in a heavy-bottom saucepan, stir to combine, and heat over a medium flame until it turns amber. Immediately pour the syrup into single portion ramekins or molds (about 3" in diameter and 2" high), coating the bottom and sides. Let cool. ● Preheat the oven to 350 °F. Combine the amaretti cookies and hazelnuts in a food processor and process until the mixture resembles fine sand. Reserve. ● In a large mixing bowl using an electric hand-held mixer, beat the eggs and sugar until creamy, then add the cocoa powder, milk, coffee, reserved amaretti-hazelnut mixture, rum and Nutella spread and beat until combined. ● Put the caramelized molds into a high-sided roasting pan. Divide the mixture among the molds, then fill the roasting pan ¾ full with hot water and bake for 30-35 minutes. ● Remove from the oven, let cool for 2 hours, then refrigerate for 3 hours before unmolding onto individual dessert plates.

Nutella passion | Puddings

Nutella passion | The Scent of Home

SEMIFREDDO WITH WARM ORANGE SAUCE

SERVES 4-6

For the semifreddo:

granulated sugar	⅓ cup	g 80
egg yolks	4	
egg whites	2	
heavy cream	1 cup	ml 250
orange zest	1	
Grand Marnier liqueur	1 T	
salt	a pinch	

For the sauce:

bitter orange marmalade	8 oz	g 200
orange marmalade	5 oz	g 150
NUTELLA® spread	½ cup	g 100
orange liqueur	2 T	
Grand Marnier liqueur	3 T	

A lovely contrast in temperatures! This cool and creamy semifreddo pairs wonderfully with the delicious warm Nutella orange sauce.

Line a loaf pan (about 8" long) with plastic wrap and reserve. ● In a bowl beat the egg yolks with the sugar until creamy and light yellow. ● In a separate bowl whisk the egg whites and salt, until stiff. ● In another bowl beat the cream until whipped. With gentle movements, first fold the whipped cream into the egg yolks and then the egg whites, zest, and Grand Marnier. Pour the mixture into the prepared pan and put in the freezer for at least 4-5 hours, until completely hardened. ● Prepare the sauce: place all the ingredients in a heavy-bottom saucepan, and heat on a low flame, stirring with a wooden spoon until creamy. ● Unmold the semifreddo onto a serving platter, remove the plastic wrap, and slice. ● Serve the warm sauce on the side.

STRAWBERRY SPOON SWEET

SERVES 6

fresh strawberries	½ lb	g 220
heavy cream	½ cup	ml 130
granulated sugar	¼ cup	g 60
NUTELLA® spread	3 T	g 50
gelatin packet	1	
juice of ½ orange		

For the strawberry sauce:

fresh strawberries plus more for garnish	¼ lb	g 100
sugar	1 ½ oz	g 40

A creamy spoon sweet that's been popular in France and Italy for centuries. Called *bavarese* there, it was named after the desserts created in the court of the princes of Bavaria in the 18th century. In this recipe it gets a fresh update thanks to the addition of Nutella.

Purée the strawberries, orange juice and gelatin powder in a blender. Reserve. ● In a bowl, whip the cream with the sugar until stiff peaks form, then slowly fold in the Nutella. ● Fold the strawberry purée into the whipped cream mixture and spoon into a ring mold. Refrigerate for 5-6 hours, until firm. ● Just before serving make the sauce: purée the strawberries and sugar in a blender until smooth. Unmold by immersing the mold for a few seconds in a bowl of hot water and then turning it quickly onto a serving platter. ● Garnish with strawberries and whipped cream and serve with the sauce on the side.

TWO-COLOR PARFAIT WITH TORRONE

SERVES 6-8

hard torrone, broken into pieces	½ lb	g 250
eggs, separated	2	
heavy cream	1 ¼ cup	ml 300
NUTELLA® spread	⅓ cup	g 70
finely ground coffee	1 t	g 5
salt	a pinch	

The French word parfait means "perfect", an apt name for this lovely dessert. The creamy white torrone contrasts beautifully with the pretty chocolatey Nutella layer.

In a food processor finely grind the torrone. ● In a bowl whisk the egg yolks for a few seconds and stir in the torrone. ● Divide the mixture between two bowls. To one, add the Nutella and ground coffee, and slowly stir until blended. ● In a large bowl, whisk the egg whites and salt until stiff. ● In another bowl, beat the cream until whipped, then fold it into the egg whites. Divide the whipped cream mixture between the two torrone bowls. ● Pour the mixture containing the Nutella into a rectangular glass dish, approx 8"x6", or if preferred a large round glass bowl. Place in the freezer for 10-15 minutes, then spread with the light-colored torrone mixture. ● Return to the freezer for at least 3-4 hours, until firm. ● Let rest at room temperature a few minutes before serving.

COFFEE PUDDING

SERVES 6

granulated sugar	⅓ cup	g 70
cornstarch	4 T	g 30
NUTELLA® spread	3 T	g 50
strong coffee, cooled	¾ cup	ml 200
lemon zest	1	
cocoa powder	1 t	g 5
water	1 cup	ml 250

This type of non-dairy pudding originated in Sicily. Here Nutella is added to the traditional coffee recipe, making a surprisingly light and refreshing treat.

Whisk the cornstarch and coffee together in a saucepan, until well blended and free of lumps. Add the sugar, cocoa powder and Nutella spread, and whisk until smooth. Stir in the lemon zest and water. ● Bring to a low boil over a low flame, stirring constantly until it thickens. Remove from the heat and pour into six small ramekins or silicone molds. ● Refrigerate for at least 6-8 hours, until firm. ● To serve, unmold onto individual dessert plates and dust with cocoa powder.

CHOCOLATE MOUSSE

SERVES 6

dark chocolate (60-70% cocoa)	4 oz	g 130
NUTELLA® spread	⅓ cup	g 90
egg yolks	2	
egg whites	3	
rum or Grand Marnier	2 T	
orange extract	6-8 drops	
salt	a pinch	

Mousse is one of the most important French culinary traditions. The name comes from the French for "foam", referring to their light and fluffy quality. This rich, but not too-sweet, treat is especially attractive served in a wine glass, but it's delicious no matter where you serve it!

Chop the chocolate and put it into a glass bowl. Melt, either in the microwave or over a pot of gently simmering water, and then stir in the Nutella. Add the egg yolks, one at a time, and stir until combined, then stir in the liqueur and orange extract. ● In a separate bowl whisk the egg whites and salt until stiff. Slowly fold into the chocolate mixture. ● Pour the mousse into wine glasses or dessert cups and refrigerate until ready to serve.

Nutella passion | Puddings

TRADITIONAL CAKES

APPLE CHARLOTTE

SERVES 6

apples	1 ¼ lbs	g 600
savoiardi,		
crisp lady fingers	½ lb (24 pieces)	g 200
NUTELLA® spread	¾ cup	g 200
blanched almonds, toasted	5 ½ oz	g 150
butter	4 T	g 60
confectioners' sugar	⅓ cup	g 60
ground cinnamon	½ t	
maraschino liqueur	½ cup	ml 100
water	½ cup	ml 100

Charlotte, the wife of George III of Hanover, was the first queen of Great Britain to have her personal residence at Buckingham Palace at the end of the 18th century. It is said that Sophia Charlotte von Mecklenburg-Strelitz (1744-1818) was particularly fond of a cold dessert made with *savoiardi* (ladyfingers) and apples. From that day on the mold used to make this cake took her name and is dedicated to her. There are records of *savoiardi* being used even earlier; they are seen in paintings from the 16th and 17th centuries hanging in the Uffizi Gallery in Florence and appear in the personal recipes of the Savoy family. According to the *Dictionnaire de Cuisine et Gastronomie* published by Larousse, in 1348 the personal cook of King Amedeo VI of Savoy prepared a spectacular dessert using "Savoyard pastry" to celebrate the official visit of the king of France.

Peel, core and finely slice the apples and place in a saucepan along with 3 tablespoons of the maraschino liqueur. Cook over a low heat for 10 minutes, then add the cinnamon and cook for another 5 to 10 minutes until soft. Let cool and pass through a fine mesh strainer and reserve. ● In a food processor, grind the almonds until they resemble fine sand. In a bowl beat the butter and sugar with a whisk until thick and light yellow. Add the almonds, apple purée and Nutella spread and stir until well blended. Refrigerate. ● Dampen the charlotte mold or 4" soufflé pan or bowl with cold water and line the bottom and up the sides with plastic wrap. ● Pour the remaining maraschino liqueur into a small bowl and dilute with water. Brush the savoiardi with the liquid and then place them side by side vertically along the length of the charlotte mold (if necessary cut off pieces of the biscuits so that they go no higher than the mold). ● Once you have covered the bottom of the mold with moistened savoiardi, top with half of the reserved apple mixture. Cover with another layer of moistened savoiardi, and then top with the remaining apple mixture. Finish with a final layer of moistened savoiardi. Cover with parchment paper and a plate to press down the layers. Refrigerate for at least 6 hours, and preferably overnight. ● To serve, unmold onto a serving plate. The charlotte may be served with a hot liqueur poured over it and then flambéed.

MONT BLANC

SERVES 6

dried chestnuts	½ lb	g 250
heavy cream	1 cup	ml 250
NUTELLA® spread	¾ cup	g 170
milk, hot	1 cup	ml 250
cocoa powder	1 oz	g 25
plus more as needed		
rum	1 T	
salt	a pinch	

A truly opulent winter dessert shaped like a snow-capped mountain, from which it gets its name. A mound of thin "spaghetti" made with a chestnut purée mixture (to which I have added Nutella), covered with whipped cream to look like snow. Created in France, it is now part of the culinary tradition of the Italian regions of Aosta, Piedmont, and Lombardy.

Soak the dry chestnuts in warm water for at least 12 hours. Drain, peel any remaining skin, place in a saucepan with 4 cups of cold water, and allow to boil, covered, for at least 50 minutes (you can reduce this cooking time by using a pressure cooker). Uncover the saucepan after 50 minutes and cook over a high flame until all the water is completely absorbed. ● Add the hot milk and salt, and slowly continue cooking until the chestnuts start to break up and the milk is absorbed. ● While still hot, mash the chestnuts by passing them through a vegetable mill or potato ricer. Put the chestnut purée into a heavy-bottomed pan along with the Nutella, rum, cocoa powder, and sugar to taste. Heat over a low flame, stirring with a wooden spoon for a few minutes to dry the mixture. ● Allow to cool slightly, and while still tepid, press the mixture once again through the vegetable mill or potato ricer and put into a bowl. Cover with plastic wrap and refrigerate for at least 5-6 hours. ● To serve: press the mixture through a vegetable mill or potato ricer to form a spaghetti-like purée onto a serving platter. Mound it to form a small "mountain". Whip the cream and place on top of the chestnut purée. Just before serving, dust lightly with cocoa powder.

Nutella passion | Traditional Cakes

AUTUMN CAKE

SERVES 6

golden delicious apples	1 lb	g 500
dried chestnuts	½ lb	g 250
NUTELLA® spread	¾ cup	g 200
amaretti cookies, crushed	¼ lb	g 100
whole milk	½ cup	ml 100
eggs	2	
Marsala wine or rum	3 T	ml 40
lemon zest	1	
salt	a pinch	
sugar, optional		

A great many traditional cakes of the mountain regions of Italy are made with chestnuts, from the Alps to the Apennines. Nutritionists have discovered that the composition of the chestnut is very similar to that of wheat; this makes its combination with Nutella particularly harmonious and agreeable. In this recipe I use boiled dry chestnuts, not chestnut flour, blended with an apple purée. The result is a delicate autumn cake, perfect for chilly evenings with friends.

Soak the dry chestnuts in lukewarm water for at least 12 hours, rinse, clean and then boil in 4 cups of water for at least 1 hour, until they are so soft that they can be mashed with a fork. Put the chestnuts through a vegetable mill or potato ricer while still hot and collect the purée in a bowl. Peel the apples, cut into small cubes, and slowly cook in a covered saucepan on a low flame for 15 minutes, if necessary adding a few drops of water. ● Take off the heat when they are completely soft. Press them through a vegetable mill or potato ricer and stir into the chestnut purée. Mix well and slowly add the Nutella, a little at a time. ● Combine the crushed amaretti and milk in a bowl and let rest a few minutes until softened. Combine the amaretti-milk mixture with the chestnut-apple purée, and add the eggs, lemon zest, Marsala, and salt. Add sugar to taste. ● Preheat the oven to 350 °F and butter and lightly flour a 9" cake pan. Pour the batter into the prepared pan and bake for about 1 hour. ● You can serve the cake warm with chocolate sauce or cold with a dollop of whipped cream.

LINZERTORTE

SERVES 6

all-purpose flour	1 ⅔ cups	g 200
butter, cold	½ cup	g 120
granulated sugar	½ cup	g 120
blanched almonds, toasted	2 ½ oz	g 65
blanched hazelnuts, toasted	2 ¼ oz	g 60
egg	1	
baking powder	1 t	g 4
ground star anise	½ t	
ground cinnamon	½ t	
ground cloves	½ t	
salt	a pinch	
raspberry jam	2 oz	g 50
NUTELLA® spread	¾ cup	g 200

Like Sachertorte, Linzertorte is considered the "pride" of the Austrian pastry-making tradition. You cannot leave Austria without tasting the delicate raspberry jam filled original version, which is from the town of Linz on the Danube, and dates as far back as 1696. In my version I've added creamy Nutella. Many claim that the best way to enjoy Linzertorte is to make it a day or two beforehand: it stays flaky and delicious for a long time.

Finely grind the almonds and hazelnuts in a food processor. ● In a large bowl beat the butter with the sugar until creamy, add the egg, almonds, hazelnuts, flour, salt, spices and baking powder. Blend quickly, using the tips of your fingers, until just combined, then form a ball. Cover with plastic wrap and refrigerate for at least 4-5 hours, and preferrably overnight. ● Using a rolling pin, roll out the dough on a lightly-floured work surface to a thickness of ¼". ● Preheat the oven to 335 °F and lightly butter and flour a 9 ½" tart pan. ● Press the dough into the pan and up the sides, pinching off any excess dough. Roll the dough scraps into a strip about 8" long and make a ring. Put the ring in the center of the tart pan, fill with the jam. Spread the Nutella on the outer circle and bake for about 30 minutes.

RICOTTA CHEESECAKE WITH PEACH JAM

SERVES 6

graham cracker crumbs	4 ½ oz	g 130
ricotta cheese	4 oz	g 125
cream cheese	4 oz	g 125
plain European-style yogurt	½ cup	g 125
peach (or apricot) jam	3 oz	g 85
NUTELLA® spread	¼ cup	g 70
butter, melted	4 T	g 60
granulated sugar	¼ cup	g 55
white corn flour	1 T	g 15
egg	1	
egg yolk	1	

There are thousands of varieties of this dessert, all of them based on ricotta or various soft cheeses. In Detroit, in the 1940s, Evelyn Torton opened a pastry shop and her cream cheese version was such a huge success that it launched a nation-wide chain of shops called the Cheesecake Factory. The base can be made with short-bread dough or crushed cookies like graham crackers. Cheese and Nutella go really well together and the peach jam adds just the right tart tang.

Put the crumbs and butter in a bowl and mix with your fingers until well combined. ● Firmly press the crumbs into the bottom and up the sides of an 8″ spring-form pan. Refrigerate for at least 20 minutes. ● Preheat the oven to 350 °F and prepare the filling: using an electric hand-held mixer beat the ricotta and cream cheese until smooth, then beat in the sugar, flour, egg and yolk. Stir in the yogurt, Nutella and jam until well combined. Pour the mixture into the prepared pan and bake for about 50 minutes. ● Let cool to room temperature, then refrigerate for at least 2 hours until completely set before serving.

HAZELNUT CAKE WITH BAROLO CHINATO ZABAGLIONE

SERVES 6

blanched hazelnuts, toasted	½ lb	g 200
granulated sugar	⅓ cup	g 80
NUTELLA® spread	½ cup	g 100
eggs, separated	4	
amaretto liqueur	2 T	ml 30
salt	a pinch	

For the zabaglione:

egg yolks	6	
granulated sugar	½ cup	g 120
NUTELLA® spread	2 T	g 30
Barolo Chinato wine	¼ cup	ml 60
ground cinnamon	a pinch	

I simply could not leave out my "pet" recipe, which reminds me so much of the hills where I was born, cloaked in vineyards and hazelnut groves. The recipe was made by my mother, Olga, who absolutely refused to use flour when making "real hazelnut cake". The Nutella gives both the cake and the Barolo-flavored zabaglione a beautiful nutty color.

Lightly butter and flour a 10" cake pan and preheat the oven to 350 °F. ● Grind the hazelnuts in a food processor until fine. ● In a bowl, using an electric hand-held mixer, beat the egg yolks and ¼ cup of the sugar until pale yellow and creamy. Slowly incorporate in the ground hazelnuts and then the Nutella and amaretto. ● In another bowl beat the egg whites, salt, and remaining sugar until stiff. Gently fold the egg whites into the batter, so as not to collapse the mixture. Pour the batter into the prepared pan and bake for about 25 minutes, until golden. ● Prepare the zabaglione just before serving: put the egg yolks and sugar into a heavy-bottomed saucepan and, using a hand-held mixer or whisk, beat until the mixture has doubled in volume and is pale yellow and thick. Very slowly add the Barolo Chinato wine, Nutella, and cinnamon, mixing carefully with a wooden spoon so as not to deflate the mixture. Put the saucepan in a bain-marie of tepid water, and cook over a low flame for 4-5 minutes until it thickens but is still frothy. ● Serve the cake with a side dollop of warm zabaglione.

Traditional Cakes | Nutella passion

HALIMA'S CAKE

SERVES 6

For the cake:

all-purpose flour	1 ⅔ cups	g 200
butter, softened	7 T	g 100
granulated sugar	½ cup	g 100
egg	1	
salt	a pinch	
baking powder	1 t	
milk	4 T	
lemon zest	1	

For the filling:

plain European-style yogurt	½ cup	g 125
egg	1	
granulated sugar	1 oz	g 30
pear	1 (large)	
NUTELLA® spread	½ cup	g 100

I ate this cake for the first time at a friend's house and couldn't stop myself from asking for the recipe, which I've gilded with the richness of Nutella. The "owner" of the original recipe is Halima, a very sweet Moroccan lady who now lives in Italy. While in Morocco, she worked for many years for a French noblewoman, who was a very good cook. From her she learned exotic dishes, but more importantly she learned the many secrets of the art of cooking, which now she so generously shares.

On a work surface sift the flour into a mound; make a hollow in the center and put in the sugar, butter, egg, milk, baking powder, zest and salt. Knead until smooth, form into a ball, cover with plastic wrap and refrigerate for 1 hour. ● Preheat the oven to 350 °F. ● Roll out the dough on a lightly floured work surface with a floured rolling pin and lay it in a 10" pie pan. Spread the bottom with Nutella. ● Peel and core the pear, cut into thin slices and lay on the Nutella in a fan-like shape. ● Using an electric hand-held mixer beat the yogurt, egg and the sugar until smooth. Pour this mixture over all the pears and Nutella. ● Bake for about 40 minutes. Allow to cool before serving.

PAVLOVA

SERVES 6

egg whites	3	
salt	a pinch	
granulated sugar	⅔ cup	g 150
confectioners' sugar	⅓ cup	g 50
potato flour or cornstarch	1 t	g 3
NUTELLA® cream	⅓ cup	g 80
heavy cream	1 cup	ml 250

A classic dessert from the beginning of the 1900s, created with layers of meringue, whipped cream and fresh fruit. As frequently happens with desserts, strangly enough more than for other types of dishes, the origin of the cake is controversial. It takes its name from the great Russian ballerina, Anna Pavlova (1881-1931), who in the '20s achieved triumphant success in Australia and New Zealand during her tours. By some accounts, this cake was first prepared in her honor in New Zealand, though it was officially dubbed "Pavlova" first in Australia. Even today the two countries dispute its origin. In this version, a chocolate lovers' delight, I've replaced the traditional fruit with Nutella. However, if you like you can still add them as garnish. Strawberries and kiwis add a particularly tasty and pretty touch. It's sure to be a success!

Preheat the oven to 225 °F. ● Prepare the meringue. Using a hand-held electric mixer, beat the egg whites and salt, until stiff, then gradually add the granulated sugar, beating until shiny. Stir in the confectioners' sugar and potato flour. ● Use three silicone molds, about 8" in diameter, or line three cake pans with parchment paper. Divide the meringue mixture into three equal parts and pour into 2 of the containers about ½" high. Delicately mix the Nutella into the remaining batter, being careful not to deflate the meringue. Pour into the last mold, and put all three meringues into the oven. ● Bake the two white meringues for 70 minutes and the Nutella one for 90 minutes. ● In the meantime whip the cream. In a separate bowl, place 2 tablespoons of Nutella and delicately fold in ⅓ of the whipped cream. Once the meringues are cooked and firm, remove from the oven and allow to cool. Gently unmold. ● Assemble the dessert within a few hours of serving: place one of the white meringues onto a serving platter and cover with half of the white whipped cream. Top with the Nutella meringue and spread with the remaining white whipped cream. Then top with the remaining meringue and cover with dollops of the Nutella whipped cream. ● It may be refrigerated for a few hours before serving.

TIRAMISU

SERVES 6

savoiardi, lady fingers	½ lb	g 200
egg yolks	6	
egg whites	3	
mascarpone cheese	1 lb	g 500
NUTELLA® spread	⅔ cup	g 140
granulated sugar	⅓ cup	g 100
strong espresso coffee	1 cup	ml 250
amaretto liqueur		
or sweet Marsala wine	½ cup	ml 100
salt	a pinch	

This easy-to-make, crowd-pleasing dessert has become world famous and is now almost an icon of Italian desserts. Notwithstanding the many "historical" stories of its Renaissance origin, in reality it was created in the Venice area in the mid 1960s when the use of mascarpone cheese became widespread.

In a large bowl, using an electric hand-held mixer, beat the egg yolks and sugar until pale yellow and creamy; slowly fold in the mascarpone. In a separate bowl whisk the egg whites and salt until stiff. Slowly fold the egg whites into the other mixture. ● In a small bowl combine the amaretto liqueur (or Marsala) and lukewarm coffee. Quickly dip some of the Savoiardi into the liquid, one at a time, and then arrange a first layer either on a serving platter or in a trifle bowl; top with the mascarpone cream, at least ½" deep. ● Put the Nutella in a pastry pouch (or syringe) with a smooth-edged opening and squeeze a fine layer over the cream. Repeat with another layer of Savoiardi and mascarpone cream. Top off with either a drizzle of Nutella or with generous dollops on the sides. ● Refrigerate, covered with plastic wrap, for at least 6 hours, preferably overnight.

PEACH PIE

SERVES 6

For the crust:

all-purpose flour	1 ½ cups	g 180
NUTELLA® spread	⅓ cup	g 80
butter, softened	4 T	g 50
sugar	1 oz	g 30
unsweetened cocoa powder	½ oz	g 15
egg	1	
salt	a pinch	
baking powder	¼ t	

For the filling:

ripe peaches, thinly sliced	2	
amaretti cookies, crushed	1 ½ oz	g 40
dark chocolate (70% cocoa)	1 oz	g 30

What would American history be without pie? Every self-respecting farmer (or farmer's wife!) of the Old West offered guests a slice of pie and a mug of steaming coffee when they came visiting. Now you find it everywhere, in fancy cafes selling drinks with Italian-sounding names, or in any of the many coffee shops and diners along the country's endless roads. In this recipe, we've added an Italian twist – Nutella in the crust! The tantalizingly delicious contrast between the tart peach filling and the buttery rich Nutella crust makes it perfect.

Prepare the crust: combine the flour, butter, cocoa powder, Nutella, egg, sugar, salt and baking powder in a food processoror bowl, and mix until just combined. Roll ⅔ of the dough into a ball and the other ⅓ into a second ball, as your bottom and top crusts. Cover in plastic wrap, and refrigerate for 1 hour. ● Preheat the oven to 350 °F. ● Roll out the larger ball of dough and line the bottom and sides of an 8" pie pan. Sprinkle with a few teaspoons of the crushed amaretti crumbs and top with the peach slices, chocolate and remaining amaretti crumbs. ● Roll out the top crust and cover. Pinch the edges closed and pierce the top with the tip of a knife in a few places. Bake for 40-50 minutes, until golden. ● Serve warm or at room temperature. ● You can substitute canned or frozen peaches for fresh, if you like.

TARTE TATIN WITH PEARS

SERVES 4-6

For the crust:

all-purpose flour	1 ¼ cups	g 140
granulated sugar	1 ½ oz	g 45
corn oil	3 T	g 35
NUTELLA® spread	¾ oz	g 20
egg yolk	1	
lemon zest	½	
salt	a pinch	
lemon juice	1 t	

For the filling:

pears	1 lb	g 400
butter	½ oz	g 15
granulated sugar	¾ oz	g 20
ground cinnamon	½ t	

The Tatin sisters of Orléans, in France, created this now world-famous dessert because of a kitchen mistake. If only the rest of us could make such "mistakes", the world would surely be a sweeter place! In my version, I've lightend the crust by substituting vegetable oil for the butter, and have added Nutella, for color and flavor. If you like, you can substitute apples for the pears. Enjoy warm with a dollop of whipped cream, if you like.

In a bowl combine the flour, sugar, oil, Nutella, yolk, zest, salt and juice and using the tips of your fingers, mix until it resembles coarse sand. ● Form into a flattened disc, cover with plastic wrap, and refrigerate for 1 hour. ● Meanwhile, peel and core the pears and cut in quarters. Slowly melt the butter in an 8" Tarte Tatin pan, or oven-proof skillet. Add the sugar and stir continuously with a wooden spoon, over moderate heat until the sugar starts to caramelize to a deep golden color. Remove from heat and place the pear quarters in a fan and slightly overlapping. Return to the heat and caramelize the pear quarters, for about 10 minutes, turning only once. Let cool and dust with cinnamon. ● Preheat the oven to 375 °F. ● On a lightly floured work surface roll out the dough with a lightly floured rolling pin so it is 1" larger than the skillet or Tarte Tatin pan. The dough should be about ⅛" thick. Place this dough over the pears, tucking it into the sides of the pie dish. ● Bake for about 30 minutes, until lightly golden. Let cool before flipping it over onto a serving platter.

Prick it, and bake it, and mark it with B,
And put it in the oven for baby and me.

OUR CHEFS

RICCARDO AGOSTINI
THE INNOVATIVE SOLOIST

Goethe wrote: «If youth be a defect, it is one that we outgrow only too soon». After nine years spent in Gianfranco Vissani's kitchen in Baschi, Riccardo Agostini has been hailed as one of the most promising young Italian chefs. And he has never wanted to have anything to do with the piadine, cappelletti and frozen fish of the *Pensione Mariuccia* on the Adriatic coast. Riccardo is a dyed-in-the-wool native of Romagna, like Federico Fellini, Arrigo Sacchi and Giovanni Pascoli. His youthful self-assurance is most definitely not a defect and continues to bolster him, now that he has no restraints in the kitchen. After two years experience as executive chef at the *Osteria del Povero Diavolo*, in Torriana, inland from Rimini, Riccardo has, since 2007, found his calling in his home town, Montefeltro in Pennabilli, which hosts not only the street theater festival in June, but also gastronomic tours. «Because», he says, «cooking is a form of expression. I wanted to be able to do it alone». And when he went to work in Vissani's kitchen in 1994? «Working with him, for me, was character forming. At first it was traumatic, because you begin on the bottom rung. Then I became his second-in-command and I realized how a dish is created. It's like going to the theater: the opening night takes place immediately, after being developed in your mind. It all starts with an ingredient, an idea...».
That is why his cuisine plays with textures and savory-sweet combinations, but always starts with excellent basic ingredients. Riccardo explains: «I think the customer is not afraid of innovative cuisine when it's made with traditional products, and I do that. I believe in simple, tasty dishes». *Il Piastrino*, which was immediately acclaimed by food critics, is the proof of that.

VENISON MEDALLIONS WITH A NUTELLA AND FOIE GRAS CORE (P. 82)

IL PIASTRINO
Via Parco Begni 5, Pennabilli (Rm)
tel. +39.0541.928106
www.piastrino.it

AIMO AND NADIA
IL LUOGO – THE PLACE OF FEELINGS

«If, in Tuscany, you were to eliminate *lampredotto* (cow's stomach stewed with tomato and sold as street food), it would be like doing away with Dante». The philosophy of Aimo Moroni, born in 1934, is summed up in this sentence. In his restaurant in Milan, where the elegance of the surroundings and his daughter Stefania's hospitality complement the excellent gourmet cooking, guests can enjoy a «cuisine with feeling», emblematic of the finest Italian tradition. It was 1955, aged twenty, that with his mother Annunziata and his wife Nadia, he opened his first restaurant, *Da Aimo*, near the central station.

Back then the dishes were *tagliatelle alla bolognese* and *giardiniera*. Today, the ingredients are more refined – black truffles with Sienese *culatello*; Ligurian bonito and pistachios; Sanremo prawns with Sicilian oranges – but the inspiration has remained the same: the feelings of a Tuscan boy in Milan with the desire to leave a trace of authenticity. And so it was. In addition to stars and awards of all kinds, the list of celebrities who have frequented *Il Luogo*, from Leonard Bernstein to Billy Joel and Bruce Springsteen, speaks for itself.

A tradition that doesn't inhibit creativity. So the combinations can change. Today, the «founding fathers», Aimo and Nadia, who have always transmitted the love that unites them and has guided their lives in the kitchen, are flanked by two chefs in their thirties, new members of the staff, Alessandro Negrini and Fabio Pisani. Sicily, Tuscany, Lombardy and Umbria – as they say in chorus – «in our restaurant, there is no place in Italy that is not represented».

SEMIFREDDO WITH NUTELLA, SOUR BLACK CHERRIES, CRUNCHY EMMER BREAD AND MOZIA SALT (P. 84)

IL LUOGO DI AIMO E NADIA

Via Montecuccoli 6, Milano
tel. +39.02.2416886
www.aimoenadia.com

LIDIA ALCIATI
A LEGEND IN THE KITCHEN

Carlin Petrini, president of Slow Food, wrote: «There is no need to be reminded of what Guido of Costigliole represented (...). He gave meaning to the words hospitality, territory, quality, commitment, words so widely shared today that they seem almost misused». It was 1961 when Guido Alciati began his extraordinary work with restaurateur Lidia Vanzini, a young woman from Costigliole d'Asti who with her mother Pierina ran another restaurant. Already back in the Seventies Guido was the forerunner of a new approach to food: a warm dining room dedicated to great cuisine, by reservation only, where the cellar held over fifty thousand bottles from around the world, and where a custom tasting menu was available.

We are in the hills of the Langhe and Monferrato, and it would not be rhetorical to mention Pavese and Fenoglio, who sang their praises. Lidia Alciati, who held Guido's flag high after her husband's untimely death in 1997, became a legend in these lands. Sadly she herself passed away in 2010, while this book was being prepared, leaving a wonderfully «widespread» family that has been fraternally united from the time the three *gagni* (kids, in dialect) in shorts began to lend a hand in the kitchen (Ugo, born in 1967), in the dining room (Andrea, born in 1971) and in the cellar (Piero, born in 1962). Lidia was at the head of a team which today has bases in Santo Stefano Belbo (Cn), Pollenzo (Cn) and Turin. From 2001, the «grandmother of all cooks» was at the Relais San Maurizio which hosts *Guido da Costigliole* in Santo Stefano Belbo, in a 17th-century convent in the Langhe hills, now a hotel and restaurant, with her son Andrea, Monica Magnini (in the dining room) and Luca Zecchin (see page 231). Lidia's veal with tuna sauce and her *agnolotti* pasta are now in the pantheon of great Italian cooking.

LIDIA'S AGNOLOTTI WITH NUTELLA (P. 86)

RELAIS SAN MAURIZIO GUIDO DA COSTIGLIOLE

Loc. San Maurizio, Santo Stefano Belbo (Cn)
tel. +39.0141.841900
www.relaissanmaurizio.it

LIDIA MATTICCHIO BASTIANICH

THE TASTE REVOLUTION

«After the sexual revolution of the Seventies, I like to think I helped the Americans carry out another social revolution, that of the palate…». Lidia Matticchio Bastianich is the «doyenne» of Italo-American cuisine. The «New York Times» has called her «a queen», though her skill, her vitality, her elegant availability to others makes her a true first lady: with the TV broadcasts (since 1998, on over 50 US stations), the books, the blog, the 18 restaurants located throughout the USA – the group of B&Bs founded with her son Joe and Mario Batali – Lidia has now reached the heights of popularity. I met her in New York in her restaurant *Felidia*, which opened in 1981, and she spoke at length, and tenderly, about Italy, which she regularly visits, Italian cuisine, which she knows incredibly well, and the evolution of Italo-American cuisine, of which she is a leading exponent.

It is charming to hear the story of the «growth of the American palate», from the time of her early cooking lessons, when she made pasta with her mother Erminia, in their house in Queens. It would take more than one novel to recount her life. Born in Pula, in the postwar period, Lidia was involved in the exodus of ethnic Italians from Istria, and arrived in New York in 1958, still a child.

After opening, with her husband Felix Bastianich, their first restaurant, *Buonavia*, in 1971, Lidia has flown solo, opening *Felidia* in Manhattan, across the Queensboro Bridge, in Mid-town. It was the beginning of a long series of successes, thanks to her shrewdness in choosing her executive chefs at *Felidia*, such as Fortunato Nicotra (see page 219), and the passion with which she continues in her work of exploration and dissemination, as a taste revolutionary.

FLAT IRON BRAISED BEEF AND SLICED GRILLED STEAK WITH PORCINI MUSHROOMS AND POLENTA TARAGNA WITH NUTELLA (P. 88)

FELIDIA

43 E. 58th St., between 2nd and 3rd Ave., New York, NY
tel. +1 212-758-1479
www.felidia-nyc.com
www.lidiasitaly.com

MATTEO BERGAMINI
A YOUNGSTER AMONG THE GREATS

«Take thought of the seed from which you spring / You were not born to live as brutes / but to follow virtue and knowledge». So wrote Dante in the 26th canto of the *Inferno*. It would certainly be superfluous to repeat this famous oration of Odysseus to his crew, to cooks of any weight. In fact for them it is important to follow a path of «knowledge», when they are young, in order to be able to reach the heights of the profession and thus lead a team. For a kitchen team resembles a Renaissance workshop, where students, by being around the teacher, learn the secrets of cooking techniques and culinary combinations.

This was the path taken by Matteo Bergamini, the young chef whom the great Tony May (see page 216) entrusted with the management of his new *SD26* restaurant in 2010. In actual fact, Matteo forged his way through the stages more quickly than most, reaching this important level of responsibility at the age of just thirty. Originally from Toscolano Maderno on the shores of Lake Garda, after studying at the hoteliers' institute he embarked on his world journey in search of «knowledge»: first in Bourg en Bresse, in France, at Alain Ducasse's La Reyssouze restaurant, to learn French secrets, and subsequently at Philippe Leveillé's *Miramonti l'Altro* in Concesio, Italy; then, from 2003, the *San Domenico* in New York under the guidance of Odette Fada. He also had a brief experience working for a Russian minister in Egypt and South Africa, until his final return to Manhattan alongside Tony May.

Now the current venture at *SD26* has completely captivated him, with a cuisine in which «the Italian tradition is not lost, and where innovative touches are added». And when he has a little spare time, Matteo loves riding his bicycle around Manhattan.

BRAISED OXTAIL WITH RADICCHIO AND NUTELLA (P. 112)

SD26
Madison Square Park, 19 East 26th Street, New York, NY
tel. +1 212-265-5959
www.sd26ny.com

MASSIMO BOTTURA
THE MEMORY ARTIST

«And suddenly the memory appeared to me. The taste was that of the piece of *madeleine* which, that Sunday morning in Combray (...), my Aunt Léonie offered me». So wrote Marcel Proust in *In Search of Lost Time*. This is what happens when you taste certain dishes at the *Osteria Francescana* in Modena: absolute reminiscences come to mind. Minimalist cuisine? No, he is an artist who knows how to concentrate the essence of a taste, making it return to the palate like a *madeleine*. Massimo Bottura is one of the leading chefs in the Italian restaurant business, a thinking chef who, as he says, «experiences cuisine in a complete, always contemporary way», looking at his Emilia-Romagna «with an improvisation of ideas» and with «total respect for the basic ingredients». Savory and sweet, hot and cold, textures and memories: Massimo plans and designs his architectural forms on the plate, starting with a *mortadella*, a cod, boiling meats which he doesn't boil.

The memory is drawn from one of those *resdore*, or housewives of Emilia – the famous cooks of the folk tradition, in the person of Lidia Cristoni who in 1987 cooked at the *Trattoria del Campazzo*, between Modena and Nonantola. It was she who taught him the art of cooking, until Alain Ducasse «discovered» him in 1992. He was impressed by him and got excited about his work, so he took him for six months to the *Louis XV* in Montecarlo. «There was so much passion, I almost got sick...», he says. Then the experience in New York, and the opening of *La Francescana* in 1996. With maturity, he developed philosophies rather than techniques regarding cuisine, so that «dreams are turned into flavors». In 2000 he began to receive the stars and hats awarded by restaurant guides. Bottura, ever vigilant, curious and quick-witted, hasn't changed. «I speak through my dishes».

NUTELLA AND BREAD (P. 90)

OSTERIA LA FRANCESCANA
Via Stella 22, Modena
tel. +39.059.210118
www.osteriafrancescana.it

Nutella passion | Our Chefs

JIMMY BRADLEY
THE MEDITERRANEAN IN NEW YORK

Just as the main character of the film *Roman Holiday*, the journalist Joe Bradley (played by Gregory Peck), loved the rustic trattorias of the Italian capital, the forty-something chef, Jimmy Bradley, is also in love with the sun and the Mediterranean. And he wants to bring them to New York. His cuisine smells of the spices of Morocco, is vivid with the light of Greece, is permeated by the flavors of southern Italy. At *The Red Cat* in Chelsea, which opened in 1999, and the more elegant *The Harrison* in TriBeCa, the cuisine is «elegant but relaxed», as the bible of Big Apple gourmets, the Zagat Guide, writes. Of his understanding of this new American cuisine inspired by simplicity, he says: «If you can create a good dish with only five ingredients, why use ten? And often, among those five, there are oil and lemon».

When you enter *The Red Cat*, in one of the most fashionable neighborhoods of Manhattan, located among art galleries and wineries with Italian names, you feel as though you were embraced by a friendly wave, which always makes the dinner enjoyable: tables close together, wood paneling and soft lighting from table lamps that lend a European flavor to the restaurant. In the kitchen, the inspiration is Italian, not slavishly, but creatively: the «asparagus risotto» uses burrata cheese; the «sauté di zucchini» and polenta uses Parmigiano cheese. Jimmy looks at you with an enigmatic smile, clear blue eyes that laugh more than the rest of his face, and recalls his New England origins, then his experience in California and Philadelphia. In TriBeCa, he has created an entirely different restaurant, more suited to a business clientele. «Because a restaurant, after all, is primarily a place where you feel good, and you want to come back».

NUTELLA AND COFFEE ICE-CREAM SUNDAE WITH COCOA NIBS, BRIOCHE CROUTONS AND CANDIED LEMON (P. 92)

THE RED CAT

227 10th Ave. (between 23rd and 24th Sts.), New York, NY
tel. +1-212-242-1122 - www.theredcat.com

THE HARRISON

335 Greenwich St. (Harrison St), New York, NY
tel. +1-212-274-9310 - www.theharrison.com

ANTONINO CANNAVACCIUOLO
THE GIANT OF FINE CUISINE

When asked about the secret of his cooking, which is of course amazingly «*bbbuona*» (as they say in Vico Equense, where he was born in 1975), he replies: «the cleanness». A quality that can be achieved, he explains, only after practicing «inner purification»: mental work that makes possible surprising dishes like «ravioli del plin alla partenopea» or «cod confit, barley and mushroom soup», where the products and the culinary traditions of the North merge with those of South. Antonino Cannavacciuolo is a giant in life and in the kitchen, and he knows how to create extraordinary dishes of exceptional delicacy.

From Sorrento, having gained experience in several important three-star French restaurants, "Tonino" landed on the shores of the romantic Lake Orta, between Piedmont and Lombardy, where in 1999, along with his wife Cinzia Primatesta – who came from a well-known family of hoteliers – he converted a 19th-century Moorish-style villa into a small, charming, luxury hotel. The spire of the house built by Cristoforo Benigno Crespi is visible from a great distance and the atmosphere in the fourteen finely refurbished rooms is magical. But the cuisine of Tonino, who has been supported for years by the talented Fabrizio Tesse, is the real star. «It's like a fire burning», says the chef. «I want to take a product to its very essence, to be able to bring out its best», he adds. When you taste his «emotions from the sea», you understand the meaning of those words.

And the Cannavacciuolo desserts are also superb: Neapolitan pastries, cannoli with ricotta cheese, puff pastries and small cakes and biscuits have lives of their own, with their own roots and ties that are never severed. In short, they are giants of goodness.

ROCHER OF RABBIT LIVER WITH NUTELLA (P. 94)

VILLA CRESPI

Via Fava, 18 Orta San Giulio (No)
tel. +39.0322.911902
www.ristorantevillacrespi.it

CESARE CASELLA
A TRUE TUSCAN IN MANHATTAN

Here is the man who brought beef rib on the bone to New Yorkers, who convinced the Americans that in France you eat well thanks to the Tuscans (a certain Catherine de' Medici...), who opened a delicatessen where the culatello was sliced on the spot, rather than in sanitized packages. This man is a "true Tuscan" (as he entitled his book of recipes), as are the cigars that have been produced for more than 150 years – with double dampening and hand-worked by cigar-makers – in Lucca, his hometown. When you talk about Cesare Casella in Manhattan you're talking about a big smile, a pat on the back, a frenzy of activities made up of events, tastings, and cookery courses.

Cesare is now the chef at *Salumeria Rosi*, an elegant Upper West Side restaurant where he has re-created – in partnership with Parmacotto and thanks to the décor of the cinema wizard, Dante Ferretti – the sparkling atmosphere of an Italian butchery. It all began in the Sixties, with his parents Peter and Rosa's restaurant-trattoria *Vipore* in Lucca, from which he has taken many of his recipes. And then in the Nineties, when still young, he began his American adventure, as executive chef at Pino Luongo's *Cuoco Pazzo*, another famous Tuscan restaurant on Madison Avenue. Later he succeeded in opening his own restaurants: first *Beppe* in 2000, then *Maremma* (both downtown), and finally, *Salumeria Rosi* in 2008.

In New York, restaurants open and close at a rate that is unimaginable in Europe, but the passion of Cesare Casella is always the same: «I want to tell the American consumer what our real products are, and oppose those who think they can fool us with false imitations. Americans are not idiots, they're much better informed now than you think...». Toscano, yes, but authentic.

BOAR IN DOLCEFORTE WITH NUTELLA
AND PAPPARDELLE PASTA (P. 96)

SALUMERIA ROSI
283 Amsterdam Ave. (73rd and 74th St.), New York, NY
tel. +1 212-877-4800
www.salumeriarosi.com

Nutella passion | Our Chefs

MORENO CEDRONI
ADRENALINE WITH THE SCENT OF THE SEA

Who is Moreno Cedroni? The chef at the elegant restaurant in front of the blue statue of the Madonnina, on the Marzocca waterfront? The life behind the informal *Clandestino suscibar* in Portonovo, Ancona and Milan? The man behind the seafood delicatessen *Anikò*? The craftsman who multiplies the goodness at *Officina*? One, nobody, and a hundred thousand, Luigi Pirandello wrote in his last novel, to describe the fragmentation of the self. Moreno looks at you with eyes the color of the Adriatic, and unruly curls, smiles and says, «Adrenaline, without that I cannot work. "Get those second courses out there", and in the kitchen, with the warmth and chaos of the team, I know I can give my best. "Get that project out there" and I know I have to succeed, with the help of my wife Mariella and all my staff. "Get that new dish out there", and I know I can rely on all my energy to be able to fly again».
Who is Moreno Cedroni? Someone who loves to score a goal with his dishes, with his unique creations, all derived from the sea which he loves as much as his job. He is a chef who avoids the obvious. It all started 24 April 1984, with an appetizer of sea snails, in the restaurant near the beach that he'd opened with a partner. Then the desire to go it alone, from 1987, the encounter with his wife, «a sweet waitress» working the summer for pocket money, and the cooking courses around the world. In two decades of «theorems and applications of taste», he has never stopped giving it his utmost. With a bandana in his hair, a multi-colored apron, a sharp curious gaze, and a wry, quiet smile, Moreno Cedroni is an artist. But with a meticulousness that is almost that of an engineer.

PIZZA WITH NUTELLA, COARSE SALT, SEA URCHIN AND CLEMENTINE OIL (P. 98)

MADONNINA DEL PESCATORE
Lungomare Italia 11, loc. Marzocca, Senigallia (An)
tel. +39.071.698267 – www.morenocedroni.it

IL CLANDESTINO SUSCIBAR, ANIKÒ SALUMERIA ITTICA, IL CLANDESTINO MILANO

ENRICO AND ROBERTO CEREA
HOSPITALITY IN THE FAMILY GENES

He would have been happy with how this country resort has taken off in Brusaporto, in the hills on the outskirts of Bergamo, and how it embodies his legacy. Vittorio Cerea, who died one autumn night in 2005, left a wife and five children who currently hold high the name of one of the best Italian restaurant families. There are two cooks, Enrico (nicknamed Chicco) and Roberto (called Bobo). Another, Francesco, is a sommelier. There are two girls: Rossella, who is head of reception (with her husband Paolo Rota, a chef alongside Chicco and Bobo), and Barbara, who manages the *Cavour* pastry shop in Bergamo (with her husband Simone Finazzi). Their father Vittorio, in 1966, had founded the previous restaurant, *Da Vittorio* in Bergamo; now 11 people are putting his teachings into practice in this hotel that has become a temple of luxury and refinement, with a kitchen of 300 square meters equipped for the preparation of both traditional dishes from Bergamo, as well as fresh fish and seafood. The arrival of the third Michelin star in 2009 has crowned an uninterrupted forty-year commitment.
Chicco and Bobo learned to handle the pans while still at school. «The passion for what we do is so great that we no longer notice the many hours spent in the kitchen». After their early apprenticeship with their father, they attended courses in France, Spain and the United States. The Cerea family are real people, working to offer guests the best possible hospitality: «Each of us has a specific task, but we remain united, because we want to continue to improve. This is our strength». The great tradition of the restaurant are the desserts, created by Enrico. «Desserts are my first love: everything comes from the fact that that I am greedy for them...».

CIABATTA WITH NUTELLA AND CARAMELIZED BANANA (P. 100)

DA VITTORIO
Via Cantalupa 17, Brusaporto (Bg)
tel. +39.035.681024
www.davittorio.com

SALVATORE DE RISO
THE GOLD OF AMALFI LEMONS

The mousse is shiny, with golden julienne. The profiteroles are white, embellished with candied peel. The delicacies with custard are decorated with a yellow tuft. Even the *tiramisu* has a scent of the Amalfi Coast. These are the desserts made with Amalfi Coast lemons, the traditional *sfusato* lemon with its elongated shape, which since 1989, Salvatore De Riso uses with love and passion. He is nicknamed the angel of sweetness and in fact he has no lack of good humor or smiles. «It's true, I owe everything to the lemon, which is my gold».

But Salvatore wasn't born a pastry chef. He started as a cook – after attending the hoteliers' institute – in the big hotels on the Amalfi Coast, full of American tourists. It was his mother, Carmela, who instilled in him the love of cooking. In 1988, after seven years in the kitchen, he realized his dream of making only desserts and pastries, and set himself up in the back of a 22 square meter bar that his father Antonio had in Piazza di Minori. That was the fortunate beginning. Now he creates new desserts, like the famous «ricotta and pears», with his reputation for delicious babàs growing, and thanks to the Accademia Maestri Pasticcieri Italiani – the Academy of Italian Master Pastry Chefs, he met Iginio Massari and many other colleagues with whom he teams up to promote Italian style in the world, to the point of becoming a TV star. Salvatore says: «I've put so much commitment and passion into succeeding, but I had all God's gifts at my disposal: citrus fruits, hazelnuts, ricotta cheese, aubergines, figs and Annurca apples».

Salvatore smiles proudly, recalling the prizes, awards and certificates that are displayed in the Tramonti workshop. Thanks to *papà* Antonio, *mamma* Carmela and lemons. *Sfusati*, if you please.

HAZELNUT PIE (P. 102)

SALDERISO

Piazza Cantilena 28, Minori (Sa)
tel. +39.089.853618
Other shops in Roma, Avellino, Pompei, Castellamare di Stabia, Nocera Inferiore and Saint Petersburg (Russia)
www.deriso.it

GENNARO AND VITTORIA ESPOSITO
A SUNNY IDENTITY

Gennaro and Vittoria: the sea of the Gulf of Naples, the Mediterranean fragrances of Campania vegetables, the sweetness of Amalfi lemons transformed into flavors. One day a cook named Alain Ducasse happened to come to the *Torre del Saracino*, a small restaurant practically on the beach. He ate the tender squid, the smooth gnocchi flavored with lemon, a tasty yellowtail and then delighted in the fig pastry. He was ecstatic. He returned to Paris and his head pastry chef and had an outburst: is it possible we're incapable of making such a good pastry? He phoned Vico Equense and Vittoria Aiello was recruited – as her husband Gennaro Esposito had been before her – and taken to France to teach them the secrets of her desserts. «Those without tricks and deceit, those that use ingredients from our area, like all of our cooking, without thickeners, transforming agents, additives and colorants», she says.

Their adventure in love&cooking began in 1992. Vittoria was 18, Gennaro 22: marriage and a restaurant all at once, swearing undying love in front of a pear soup with millefeuille. Vittoria says: «My father owned a restaurant nearby, and advised us to open a new one for ourselves. The French star was awarded after three years, but the real satisfaction was when that famous chef came here and told me that my dessert was divine».

Gennaro says: «Cooking is a passion, an identity. I learned to cook the ingredients of this land that I love, using technique, knowledge, and culture». In the space of just a few years the small room inside a Saracen tower has become one of the best restaurants in Italy. And each year, in Vico, the greatest Italian chefs meet up for a big friendly party by the sea.

MILLEFEUILLE OF HAZELNUT CREAM AND NUTELLA (P. 104)

TORRE DEL SARACINO

Via Torretta 9, Vico Equense, Marina di Seiano (Na)
tel +39.081.8028555
www.torredelsaracino.it

Nutella passion | Our Chefs

GINO FABBRI
CAKES ARE A MESSAGE OF LOVE

Gino Fabbri, pastry chef-gentleman with a smiling face and the mellow speech typical of Emilia, has interpreted McLuhan, believing in only one tool of communication: cakes. He produces a large quantity of them in his workshop in the artisans' area of Bologna. «We have to live up to what the customers demand: a birthday, a happy moment in their lives, a traditional celebration with a party, a way of saying "I love you" to a person who is dear. And for this we must leave the bakery and go to the bar/pastry shop, talk to those who come into the store for a moment of sweetness, understand their needs. Yes, a cake is always an important message, more than any other dessert».

On the workshop's sign and on the elegant packaging, with minimal graphics, he now has his own name, *Gino Fabbri Pasticciere*, but until 2003 he had found a more impish company trademark – *La Caramella* (The Candy) – to identify the business he started in 1982.

He has had his hands in cream and chocolate since he was a boy. Even today – he is now at the top of the profession as vice-president of the Academy of Italian Master Pastry Chefs – that dedication has not faded: with humility he is always ready to challenge his fellow pastry cooks and always demands that the basic ingredients used be of exactly the same standard as the creativity. «I want to convey the image of quality, make it clear that this is our daily effort», he says. If it is true that his profession, as he says, «catches the eye», his creations are also made for giving pleasure to the eye and the palate. Fundamentally, Gino's message is a messge of love, passion and a bit of fun. «I always repeat to young people: you have to have imagination and creativity, but you also have to make them smile».

SWEET MEMORY CAKE (P. 106)

PASTICCERIA GINO FABBRI

Via Cadriano 27/2, Bologna
tel. +39.051.505074
www.ginofabbri.com

GUIDO MARTINETTI AND FEDERICO GROM
CONES OF YESTERYEAR

Eggs, fresh milk, cream, brown sugar and cocoa solids from Ecuador. These are the high-quality basic ingredients used for the basic flavors: *fiordilatte*, the "cream of yesteryear", and extra dark chocolate. For other specialties: coffee from the highlands of Huehuetenango Guatemala, Piedmont Tonde e Gentili IGP hazelnuts, acacia honey, cornmeal Battifollo cookies, fresh fruit from the Mura Mura estate in the Monferrato hills. They have named it *Grom il gelato come una volta* (the ice-cream of yesteryear) and in May 2003 they opened the first shop in Turin, just a short walk from the Porta Nuova station. They chose a bar with *carapine*, the deep buckets for keeping ice-creams well chilled and covered with protective lids, instead of visible trays. And now long queues of patient admirers are forming.

A winning formula, which in just a few years has led to many more ice-cream parlors in many Italian cities, and then in Paris, New York, and Tokyo. They are served by a central hyper-technological workshop: the bags with liquid creams are transported in refrigerator trucks, then made up in the individual shops at the appropriate moment. The business was started by two friends in their thirties: Guido Martinetti, who deals with basic ingredients, production and communication, and his business partner, Federico Grom, who handles administration and staff management. They explain: «Italy is world famous for ice-cream, but very few produce it using the old quality artisan criteria: there is plenty of room for this type of activity». With their arrival, the «cold art» is back in fashion. It all started in high school, as Guido confesses: «I have always been crazy about ice-cream. I used to ask the girls home to get them to try my dark chocolate *stracciatella*: it was a better excuse than a butterfly collection…».

NUTELLA ICE-CREAM AND ITS ELEMENTS (P. 108)

GROM

Piazza Paleocapa 1/d, Torino
tel. 011.5119067 and in other streets – www.grom.it
New York, NY: 2165 Broadway (and 76th), Upper West Side;
233 Bleecker Street (and Carmine), Greenwich Village;
1796 Broadway

IGINIO MASSARI
THE MASTER OF MASTERS

Saccharomyces cerevisiae. The fungus that thousands of years ago was "kidnapped" by men for the production of wine, beer, bread and all the doughs and batters used for making desserts. Without baker's yeast there would be no croissants, no *panettone*, no brioches. And there would be no one to master it, no Iginio Massari. Without the knowledge of yeast there would be no pastry-maker's art. Iginio Massari is the first Italian member of the international association Relais Dessert (1985), the founder of the Academy of Italian Master Pastry Chefs (1993), and Italian champion in the World Pastry Chefs' Competition in Lyon (1997): without him, the history of the art of Italian pastry-making would have been quite different.

Iginio, a powerful and athletic man, is from Brescia. He is the soul of a group of exceptional white jackets, who stimulates but never spares anyone. His own passion was roused by the *casoncelli*, the typical candy-shaped ravioli from Brescia – hand prepared by his mother, with the thinnest of pasta – and the aroma of soup from the family restaurant.

In 1971, at the age of thirty, with his wife Mari he opened the *Veneto* pastry shop in Brescia, one of the purest examples of the pastry-making art in Italy. If you ask Iginio Massari what his favorite kind of pastry is, he replies without any hesitation: «Il panettone, la colomba, il pandoro (special sweet cakes for Christmas and Easter holidays). Not because they are associated with festivities, but because they are made with a leavened dough that requires a long baking process: you have to add the waiting time to the basic ingredient and the pastry-making skill». For Massari, there are no boundaries between sweet and savory, all that really matters is the difference between good and mediocre: «The most important thing is to have enough knowledge to perform this job well».

NUTELLA SOUFFLÉ (P. 110)

PASTICCERIA VENETO
Via Salvo D'Acquisto 8, Brescia
tel. +39.030.392586
www.iginio-massari.it

Nutella passion | Our Chefs

TONY MAY
THE AMBASSADOR OF MADE IN ITALY

To mention Tony May in New York City is to speak of a flag bearer for Italian food, a man who has dedicated fifty years of his life to quality restaurants, who has tried to make people forget that stereotyped image of our restaurants with the checkered tablecloths of Little Italy. Today he leads the GRI, Group of Italian Restaurateurs in North America, and is owner, with his daughter Marisa, of the renovated and elegant *SD26* – three floors decorated by Massimo Vignelli where you can eat or drink something at all hours – reopened in 2009 as an ideal continuation of his famous *San Domenico*. Antonio Magliulo can rightly say that he has made it. Not only demonstrating what genuine Italian cuisine is, but also providing living proof of how a young man aged 26 arriving in America, in 1963, can start out as a waiter and end up being a restaurant entrepreneur.

Born in Torre del Greco, the first of eight children, Tony worked his way through the ranks to become owner, in the space of a single decade, of the *Rainbow Room* in the Rockefeller Center. It was also the time of his first Italian restaurant, the *Palio* (1986), then the *San Domenico* (1988-2008), *Gemelli* and *Pasta Break* (1997, unfortunately the Twin Towers were destroyed by the September 11 attack, but fortunately the staff was evacuated in time), and finally *SD26*. Commendatore May is not yet satisfied, despite the personal success he has achieved with books and television broadcasts. He is currently engaged in a new battle: «against counterfeit Italian cuisine, a victim of its own success in the United States. What counts are authentic recipes with original products, which have to be interpreted by Italian chefs...». A true ambassador, sometimes without too much diplomacy, defending the "Made in Italy" brand.

BRAISED OXTAIL WITH RADICCHIO AND NUTELLA (P. 112)

SD26
Madison Square Park, 19 East 26th Street, New York, NY
tel. +1 212-265-5959
www.sd26ny.com

FABRIZIA MEROI
DOLOMITES À LA CARTE

The naturalist Déodat del Dolomieu studied the rocks of these mountains in the late 18th century. Who knows if the French scientist ever stayed at Sappada, in the heart of the Dolomites, in the wooden house built back then but which now houses Roberto Brovedani and Fabrizia Meroi's restaurant. When you arrive up here in summer you will experience the scent of herbs gathered from the meadows around the village, while in winter the heat of the *stube* releases ancient humours from the timbers of the old house. Fabrizia Meroi is one of the most talented female chefs of the *Jeunes Restaurateurs d'Europe*, an association of which the two owners of *Laite* have been members since 1997, when the restaurant was not yet in the current and sophisticated place it is now. And to think, as they shyly like to tell, that they met when very young, he working in the dining room of a restaurant and she in the kitchen washing dishes. They have come a long way together, always with modesty and hard work: he with his passion for the wine cellar, which he manages with great professionalism, and she in the kitchen with increasingly intriguing and perfect combinations and techniques.

The cuisine at *Laite* thus reflects the influences of the surrounding territory, though is not conditioned by it: it can be a pleasant surprise for the palate to taste the potato ravioli or juniper tortellini with an innovative filling of grilled guinea hen and a delicate sauce of green asparagus. The Dolomites unfold just as the menu does, with lightness and levity, in this award-winning mountain restaurant. Right down to the famous *prato* for dessert, in which the land is represented by chocolate: a dish that leaves sweet memories of Roberto and Fabrizia.

MILLEFEUILLE OF SMOKED FOIE GRAS WITH NUTELLA AND CHERRIES (P. 114)

LAITE
Borgata Hoffe 10, Sappada (Bl)
tel. +39.0435.469070
www.ristorantelaite.com

FORTUNATO NICOTRA
THE RIGOR OF AUTHENTICITY

When Fortunato and Lidia decide what dishes to put on the menu, they discuss a recipe, they explain what they mean by «authentic Italian food», and their eyes shine with a different light. They understand each other at a glance. She is from Friuli; he is from Sicily. But they share a love for Italy that they know how to transfer to the menu of *Felidia*, Lidia Bastianich's restaurant where Fortunato Nicotra came to work as executive chef in 1995. He was already behind two starred restaurants in Sicily and important experiences in Piedmont, where he studied at the Colombatto Hotelier Institute in Turin. Their professional understanding was so immediate that it convinced the young talent from Baucina, a small town in Palermo where he was born in 1962, to stay on in New York.

It was a well considered choice, as Nicotra explains: «the real turning point was Sicily. After studying in Turin, a city I had gone to as a child and to which I am still very attached, and a brief stint in Germany, my first personal achievements were at the restaurant *Villa Marchese*, near Messina, which was opened in 1985 by Franco Marzini. I was able to work with the freshest ingredients, the place was fantastic and creativity could unfold in search of authenticity. It is the same commitment we have here at *Felidia*, seeking the renewal of Italian products and Italian cuisine with a lighter and more modern style».

Fortunato Nicotra quickly became a star in the United States, thanks to the Iron Chef television show and Lidia's books, in which he actively collaborated. Thanks to his cuisine, the American magazine «Wine Spectator» has added *Felidia* to the top ten Italian restaurants in the United States.

FLAT IRON BRAISED BEEF AND SLICED GRILLED STEAK WITH PORCINI MUSHROOMS AND POLENTA TARAGNA WITH NUTELLA (P. 88)

FELIDIA
43 E. 58th St., between 2nd and 3rd Ave., New York City
tel. +1.212-758-1479
www.felidia-nyc.com

Nutella passion | Our Chefs

DAVIDE PALLUDA
THE BEAUTY OF THE TERROIR

To the left of the Tanaro, the river that descends from the Maritime Alps in Piedmont to the Po, there is a chain of more jagged hills amid the softer hills of the Langa: for some years now they have been the pilgrimage destination for gourmands. Canale is at the heart of this *terroir*, and the Roero restaurant: not just bottles of wine, but also a wine bar, the *Enoteca*, which over the years has become a reference point for quality restaurants. From the beginning, as chef and owner, in that restaurant, there is a young man who knows how to interpret cuisine with a strong personality. «It must express a message of territoriality, which does not mean a tradition that is an excuse to stand still». Davide Palluda is a child prodigy who has been learning the culinary art since 1988 – not even an adult – in that great forge of a restaurant, *Felicin* in Monforte d'Alba, also gaining experience in Germany, France, and Liguria.

Davide has been at the *Enoteca* since 1995, where he is assisted by his sister Ivana, who manages the dining room, but he loves coming to talk with customers, with his eternally cheerful charm, easy-going smile, and a joke at the ready. For him, cooking has always had a playful side, and this is evident in one of his much-imitated dishes, «fassone beef from head to toe». In recent years he has also developed his own line of products, from fondue to sauces and jams.

Above all, Palluda is convinced that the chef has a duty: «to create his own personality and know how to convey it. Otherwise what happens is what happens with so many young people today, going from one job to another, working six months in the best places, with restaurateurs with great charisma, but when faced with the menu, they don't know how to fill it». Davide's elegant and refined desserts are the result of this theorem: joy, a sunny approach, passion.

GLAZED APRICOTS FILLED WITH NUTELLA (P. 116)

ENOTECA
via Roma 57, Canale (Cn)
tel. +39.0173.95857
www.davidepalluda.it

MARCO PARIZZI
CREATIVITY "ALLA PARMIGIANA"

«... And there was a mountain of grated Parmesan cheese....». In his description of Bengodi, the land of plenty, in the middle of the 14th century, Boccaccio sings the praises of that most famous of all Italian cheeses. «I offer it in its various stages of maturity, from 12 to 24 to 36 months: along with cured meats and wine, it is the only product that is not made in my kitchen». Marco Parizzi is speaking. He is a true Parmesan with very clear ideas about what dishes to make in his lovely restaurant in the center of the Emilian city. «Nothing is pre-prepared, it's all homemade, from the bread to the desserts». He is from a family of cooks: his grandfather was the innkeeper of the *Tiratardi* trattoria and his father Ugo re-established the family restaurant, moving and renaming it *Parizzi* in 1956, winning a Michelin star in the Seventies.

Father Ugo ran the restaurant and he helped him in the dining room. «I worked for pocket money and cooking didn't attract me yet». He started cooking when his father told him that the cook he'd hired would be leaving. However, Marco hated «the repetition of certain dishes, always the same. I found the system for innovating the cuisine by inviting up-and-coming chefs to work with us, like Davide Oldani, Claudio Melis and the Frenchman Patrick Masera. From the latter, especially, I learned so much...».

In 1994 the management of the restaurant passed into his hands. Since then there have been awards for a modern cuisine whose strong points are its creative lightness and the excellent basic ingredients. Marco Parizzi, with his wife Cristina in the dining room, continues to have clear ideas: «I hate it when people talk about "revisited" food. For me, the flavor is essential, not culinary techniques or aesthetics taken to the extreme. My recipes are full of flavor, without compromises».

BITTERSWEET WITH CRUNCHY NUTELLA (P. 118)

PARIZZI
Via della Repubblica 71, Parma
tel: +39.0521.285952
www.ristoranteparizzi.it

GIANCARLO PERBELLINI
THE KING OF DESSERTS

For at least three generations, in Veneto and in Italy, the name "Perbellini" has been synonymous with the art of desserts. In 1891 Giovanni Battista Perbellini invented the *Pandoro* of Verona: the name was later used by big industry, but the family has maintained its original recipe and still makes the *Offella d'oro* – the golden cake. Giovanni's son Ernesto then created the *Millefoglie Strachin*, made with a sweet dough rolled thin and stuffed with a soft cream made from milk, eggs, butter, sugar, and vanilla. Today, the forty-year old Giancarlo Perbellini represents the fourth generation of this family of dessert makers. Unlike his baker father Titta, who still helps in the kitchen, Giancarlo wanted to be a chef. His first experiences were in Italy and Europe (*Taillevent*, *Ambroise*, *Terrasse* in France, *San Domenico* in Imola, *Desco* and *12 Apostoli* in Verona). Then in 1989 he opened a restaurant that bears the family name in Isola Rizza, a small town not far from Verona and Bovolone, where the workshop and pastry shop are located.

In the space of just a few years, the restaurant *Perbellini* has reached the heights of the Italian restaurant business. The chef explains: «In the kitchen, seasonal products are very important for me, but I want to keep the tradition going». Thus, dishes were created in which there is a main ingredient that supplies the underlying theme, like the famous «*colori e sapori del mare* – colors and flavors of the sea», including appetizers, or *ravioli* stuffed with tomato, a true surprise for the palate. But it is in the endless merry-go-round of delicious cakes that every sweet lover can find satisfaction, with forty different desserts on offer: from the Strachin with caramelized gingerbread and golden apricots, to the chocolate sphere and the ricotta mousse, or the fruit salad, the sorbets, the great sweets trolley, an assortment fit for a king.

BREAD, PIGEON, NUTELLA AND FOIE GRAS (P. 120)

PERBELLINI
Via Muselle 130, Isola Rizza (Vr)
tel. +39.045.7135352
www.perbellini.com

VALERIA PICCINI
MAREMMA INSTINCT

Dante called it «Corneto», that wilderness between Tuscany and Lazio which everyone now knows as the Maremma. We must leave behind the Tyrrhenian Sea and climb to the ancient village of Montemerano, in the direction of Lake Bolsena, to find the sign for this place, *Caino*, the realm of the Menichetti family since the Seventies. At that time, when it opened, it was a tavern serving wines: Angela and Carisio ("Caino" to his friends) opened it and seven years later Valeria Piccini went to work there, and after a time married their son Maurizio. As Valeria loves to recall, it was immediately a home and workplace: «First, my husband showed me the kitchen, then he married me...».

In 1987, following the death of Carisio, the young couple were alone at the helm of the restaurant and decided to renew it thoroughly, with new dishes, a larger dining room, a cuisine in which traditional food was enhanced by new techniques that made it lighter. Valeria and Maurizio, who are especially passionate about the winery, are beginning to travel Europe to learn about the best restaurants, taking lessons from their examples. And there has been success: the first Michelin star in 1991, and the second in 1999.

Even today, it is a substantial cuisine. «Keeping it simple, as I express myself through my dishes, does not mean halting my creativity, but trying to get close to what I call the "right taste", so that our guests can feel all the passion and love we've put into preparing a menu», says Valeria. All this without forgetting what is called «instinct» at *Caino*. Thanks to instinct, a favorite dish was created, the Cinta Senese ravioli with chicken broth, chestnuts and baby vegetables with balsamic vinegar: the pork flavor contrasting with the sweetness of the chestnuts...

NUTELLA CHOCOLATE, LICORICE AND EXOTIC FRUIT (P. 122)

CAINO
Via Canonica 3, Montemerano (Gr)
tel. +39.0564.602817
www.dacaino.it

Nutella passion | Our Chefs

GIOVANNI PINA
CREAM PUFF THERAPY

«There's a little child inside us, who not only does not tremble (...) but still has tears and jubilations». Giovanni Pascoli wrote this in *Il fanciullino* (The Young Child). It would certainly not be inappropriate to use this quotation in presenting Giovanni Pina, pastry chef at Trescore Balneario, a thermal spa not far from Bergamo, where his family have been pastry-makers for three generations. It is he who reminds us, trying to explain why one day, when he was a university student, having faced the possibility of becoming an oncologist, he decided to stay in the workshop of his father Mario, where his grandfather Giovanni had been making pastry since 1920. «I pictured myself running around behind the head physician. I told myself it would be nicer to give joy to people with a sugar sculpture, see their smiles, rediscover the children within them, as Pascoli wrote...».

Maybe it was because, in the family, there had been a great grandfather whose first name was Ricciotti (like the patriot Nicola, who was shot with the Bandiera brothers) and was a fervent partisan on the side of Garibaldi, but Gianni Pina does not face life with apathy. Nor is this a medical failure. Now he is an accomplished baker. During his career in pastry-making, he had a decisive meeting with Iginio Massari, whom he succeeded in 1999 as president of the Academy of Italian Master Pastry Chefs.

Gianni Pina's personal therapy for inducing happiness is certainly not based on analgesics or antibiotics, but cream puffs, cookies, cakes and panettone – a sweet festive bread. Mindful of that nickname given to the Pina family – «the Ricciotti» or «the Ciotti» – he has been creating pastries for some time, made of corn meal and called... well... «Ciotti». Pascoli would have approved.

SMILE (P. 124)

PASTICCERIA PINA
Via Locatelli 14, Trescore Balneario (Bg)
tel. +39.035.940344
www.pasticceriagiovannipina.it

VITO POLOSA
AROMA OF BASILICATA

Grilled octopus, baked linguine, grilled lamb and "gianduia panna cotta": one could almost be in Italy, reading the menu of *Aroma Kitchen & Winebar*, in downtown Manhattan. Vito Polosa, a young chef born in 1972 in Acerenza in Basilicata, with his wife Alessandra, did everything to bring the "flavor" of Italian food to his restaurant in New York in 2005.
Because he has breathed in the scent of real flavor since his childhood, when he went out into the countryside to press olives at his grandfather's mill, Vito says, with a smile: «The farmers came to us to get their olives pressed and in return they gave us wine, so I specialized in wine. I wanted to open a winery. I thought it would be a pleasant experience in

life...».

He was little more than twenty, in 1993, when he arrived in New York on vacation to visit his brother. He was supposed to visit for a month, but it turned into a permanent stay. And he began working as an assistant cook in various restaurants, until he decided to take the plunge and go it alone. Today his small and romantic restaurant has become very fashionable among young Americans, who know they can find a true and honest dish of Italian cuisine, as well as excellent wine labels: it is furnished with a few tables on the ground floor, a reserved room in the cellar and a lot of good feeling, from behind the bar as well. Vito and Alessandra (originally from Malta) both say: «We love the land and its products and our childhood in the Mediterranean was always influenced by it: there were those big family tables where the food was a very important moment for being together. We want to convey this pleasure to everyone». With the right flavor!

NUTELLA SEMIFREDDO (P. 126)

AROMA KITCHEN & WINEBAR

36 East 4th St. (East Store), New York, NY
tel. +1 212-375-0100
www.aromanyc.com

NICOLA AND PIERLUIGI PORTINARI
THE HALLMARK OF AUDACITY

In Veneto there is a town – between Verona and Vicenza, at the foot of the Berici Hills – called Lonigo. Once there were three sisters with an inn, which, since 1987, has been managed by two brothers, Nicola and Pierluigi, whose family name is Portinari. To inaugurate the new restaurant the two boys, not yet thirty, decided to do as the French maid Babette did in the novel by Karen Blixen. One day Babette said to her employers, Martina and Filippa, «Mesdames, let me give my best». Nicola and Pierluigi had not won the lottery, as she had, but in 1988 they offered lunch to the entire town. They had decided to name their new restaurant *La Peca*, which in Venetian means "impression" or "mark". After that, as in the village of the famous opening lines of *Babette's Feast* – «in Norway there is a fjord named Berlevaag» – everyone knew what good cooking is. «Traditional flavors with true audacity», as the Spanish of «Lo Mejor» wrote of them.

Nicola is in the kitchen, while Pierluigi looks after the dining room, with major incursions into the kitchen for dessert. They say, «tradition and memories should be interpreted, while the flavors remain intact, in their essence». And when, in the hills around the restaurant, the old women of the village gather herbs from the fields, the *La Peca* menu changes, there are scents of those plants, they adapt, as during periods when there are new Rotzo potatoes or the hard-to-come-by *zotoli*, the microscopic cuttlefish from Chioggia. In his desserts, Pierluigi always gives an impression of innovation: «We must offer moments of instant pleasure, which should be light». Professionalism, technique and passion are their true hallmark, and it stays in the heart. Audacity, yes, but with feet well on the ground.

NUTELLA SANDWICHES WITH TANGERINE JELLY, SZECHWAN PEPPER AND SAFFRON YOGURT CREAM (P. 128)

LA PECA

Via Giovannelli 2, Lonigo (Vi)
tel. +39.0444.830214
www.lapeca.it

Nutella passion | Our Chefs

ANTONELLA RICCI
A DOUBLE BURNER

Everything started in 1967 around the traditional "burner" used for cooking the skewers of beef sausages, the *marri* (rolls made from lamb's intestine) and *agnellone* (sheep) with onions: a fire that must stay lit for hours and then smoulder with coals to cook the meat in the best way. Apulian tradition that has become famous in this small restaurant in Ceglie, a major agricultural center in Salento. Angelo Ricci served in the dining room, his wife Dora was in the kitchen. Their daughter Antonella, while studying and graduating in political sciences, gave a hand, watched and learned the trade.

It has been almost twenty years and that girl is now one of the most promising and lively chefs of the *Jeunes Restaurateurs d'Europe*, because she has succeeded in transforming the family concern. The *orecchiette* pasta, sliced cured meats and leg of kid are still there, but the Mediterranean scents and herbs have been mixed with other more exotic flavors: vanilla, curry, and pepper. *Il Fornello* has now expanded to become a multiethnic experience, with the fusion cuisine just mentioned. It all began in 1998. Antonella, not yet thirty, went to the Mauritius Islands for a week dedicated to Italian cuisine in some large hotels. There she got to know a promising young chef named Vinod Sookar.

And so began their tale of love, crowned by marriage, and the decision to stay together in the kitchen, always faithful to the traditions of Apulia, like the famous meatballs at the beginning of each menu or the Ceglie biscuits at the end. Antonella and Vinod explain: «We're a young couple, in our dishes we like to experiment with flavors from around the world...». Mother Dora oversees in the kitchen, while sister Rosella, between concerts, handles the wine and hospitality with professionalism.

ZUCCHINI FLOWERS STUFFED WITH RICOTTA AND NUTELLA IN A WARM RUM SAUCE (P. 130)

AL FORNELLO DA RICCI
Contrada Montevicoli, Ceglie Messapica (Br)
tel. +39.0831.377104
www.ricciristor.it

ROBERTO RINALDINI
PRET-À-PORTER SWEETS

His creations, sugary and scented with muscatel raisins and honey, will never run the risk that Charles Baudelaire outlines when he describes bad luck in the *Fleurs du mal* (*Le guignon*): «*maint joyau dort enseveli / dans les ténèbres et l'oubli*» (Many a jewel lies buried in darkness and oblivion). Certainly no oblivion for Roberto Rinaldini and his rows of «desserts à porter», works of art in chocolate, sugar and fruit. Sweets to look at before being sweets to eat, which he sells in a small boutique in the center of Rimini. Roberto, who was very young when he went to study at the Academy of Italian Master Pastry Chefs, quickly became famous. He has applied the laws of glamor to the art of pastry-making and every six months presents his collections, prepared with his wife Nicole. In 2006, with Colalucci and Tonon, he won the World Cup in ice-cream making, having already received several awards in Barcelona, Lyon, and Luxembourg.

«This job is my life now. I love it in all its nuances. And my ambition is to be able to make all my creations good-tasting and good-looking in an innovative way», says Roberto. His father, a hotelier in Rivabella, being a practical man, gave Roberto an either/or ultimatum when he was 18 years old: get a real job. «Maybe volleyball, which I played as a boy, has lost a star athlete, but I gained from it. I went on to apprentice in pastry-making and took my new job with a sporting spirit, trying to win...».

And so it was. Since 2000, with the hotel closed, Rinaldini began to knead, bake, and decorate pralines and little pastries. «We work from five in the morning until eight in the evening, we train for international competitions, and we try to grow without being conditioned by the Romagna Riviera, but with an eye on the world».

NUTELLA PIADINA (P. 132)

PASTICCERIA RINALDINI
Via Coletti 131, Rimini
tel. +39.0541.27146
www.rinaldinipastry.com

NIKO ROMITO
A SMILE IN THE MOUNTAINS

«I like cooking: with a product, you can create a dish that wins a person over and touches them. The work of the chef is very delicate. We manipulate something that others ingest. And when a guest has eaten well, I know from the way he or she looks at me». From the expression in Niko's large hazel eyes one can tell that his decision to be at the stove is intentional. He could have joined a professional studio after studying economics and business in Rome. But instead he stayed in Rivisondoli, his home town perched 1300 meters up in the Abruzzi mountains, where his father Antonio handed down his love for food: there, he is still looking for the smile that he could see on Sunday customers' faces, before the pastry shop opened, and later the family restaurant. In 1995, a small restaurant was opened there called *Reale*, in honor of the noble building in which it is housed. When their father passed away, Niko and his sister Cristina, with a considerable dose of courage and optimism, decided to continue the family business in the world of haute cuisine. After completely renovating the restaurant, in 2000 Niko began climbing the ladder to success and international fame, having barely reached the age of thirty.

«My cooking is simple, with few ingredients, but I want it to be both explosive and harmonious. Niko smiles when he remembers the student from Abruzzo who one day decided to take a cookery course in Rome. In the space of just a few years, Niko has arrived at the very top of the Italian restaurant business, has been awarded two Michelin stars, won numerous prizes and earned flattering praise from the First Ladies of the G8 conference, held in L'Aquila in 2009, when he cooked for them. «Starting from nothing, for me it was an unexpected explosion...», he confides today.

NUTELLA, BREAD AND FENNEL (P. 134)

REALE
Viale Regina Elena 49, Rivisondoli (Aq)
tel. +39.0864.69382
www.ristorantereale.it

ALFREDO RUSSO
A NEW STYLE IN THE PALACE

Joy, anguish, the passion of love, with a hint of something unspoken and poetic. This is what the *stilnovisti* – the new style artists – wanted for Italian literature in the middle of the 13th century. Like Dante in the 24th canto of *Purgatorio*, Alfredo Russo wanted to adopt this poetic expression to describe his cuisine. He feels like an innovator with respect to the past, though he still has roots in Piedmont. After years of success at Ciriè, in the Canava area, from September 2008 the *Dolce Stil Novo* is housed in the East Tower of the beautifully restored castle of Venaria Reale. Alfredo added *alla Reggia* (at the Palace) to the original name and won the favor of even more customers and critics, in a dining room where his wife Stefania is a dedicated reception hostess.

Alfred Russo believes that cooking is a kind of «inner need», associated with the ingredients one handles. It is the spontaneity that can suddenly arise from a particularly flavorful tomato, or a fish that has come from the sea with a livelier eye than usual.

«I want to succeed in conveying a bit of joy and fun with my dishes. I always put a "surprise" on the menu for customers. If we don't enjoy ourselves, then the customers cannot enjoy themselves either», he says, with those dark eyes that denote a family from Puglia. Alfredo Russo's cuisine is evolution, movement, and lightness. And his great passion is desserts. At his table one can taste up to ten in rapid succession. In these delicacies is a search for textures, aromas, scents that play above all with chocolate. «They are conceived as non-sweet sweets, with delicate contrasts and a rather "special" style». Always new.

BREAD AND NUTELLA (P. 136)

DOLCE STIL NOVO ALLA REGGIA
Piazza della Repubblica 4, Venaria (To)
tel. +39.011.4992343
www.dolcestilnovo.com

PAOLO SACCHETTI
FROM THE PEOPLE'S CLUB TO THE NEW WORLD

His story might have inspired Nanni Moretti to write some scenes for the «musical about a Trotskyist pastry-maker in the conformist Italy of the 1950s», a film he never shot, despite having announced it in his film *Caro Diario* (Dear Diary). The location is between the towns of Figline Valdarno, Sesto Fiorentino and Prato. The story begins in the countryside, where there is a greedy little boy who loved to *strogolare* – mess around with garden vegetables and fresh eggs. At the age of 16 his father sent him to learn the trade. After a few years, he opened the pastry shop *Rinascita* in a Casa del Popolo (a popular recreation and meeting place). The story ends happily in Prato in 1989, when he opened a workshop with a window display in the center of town: the place was called *Nuovo Mondo*, a different era for cantucci, ricciarelli, panforte, and schiacciatina. The story is that of Paolo Sacchetti, vice president of the Academy of Italian Master Pastry Chefs. «They were years of hard work, and even now I have to get up at five in the morning and go on until eight at night, Sundays included. But I'm not one of those company owners who likes staying in the workshop. I like to be out "front", even if my wife is already there, as my partner. I'm interested in seeing customers and hearing what they think about my desserts». Paolo Sacchetti is very demanding: he personally selects the basic ingredients. «For me, born in the country, eggs, milk, cherries and apricots are valuable assets, they improve my product. With me, you'll never find a dessert out of season». If he's not the Trotskyist pastry chef Moretti is looking for, he undoubtedly has something in common with the Roman film-director: that scooter he bought himself as a boy with money earned by apprenticing in the pastry shop in the Casa del Popolo, where he began his sweet adventure towards... a new world.

CLAFOUTIS WITH PEARS AND NUTELLA (P. 138)

PASTICCERIA CAFFÈ NUOVO MONDO

Via Garibaldi 23, Prato
tel +39.0574.27765

VITTORIO SANTORO
THE PEDAGOGY OF THE PROFITEROLE

You have to take the ring road at Brescia and continue on to the industrial area to understand who Vittorio Santoro is. Since 1997, in the midst of gleaming work surfaces in rooms with ultra-modern ovens and refrigerators, leading professionals of the culinary art have taken it in turns to train cooks, pastry chefs, chocolatiers, and ice-cream makers... A pedagogy of the profiterole arising from a project created by the president of the Academy of Italian Master Pastry Chefs, Iginio Massari, who found in Vittorio an exceptionally professional collaborator. Thousands of students have passed through that building on the outskirts of Brescia, young trainees and established professionals seeking the latest in Art, Science, and Food Technology, as the *Cast* is defined.

Vittorio is one of those «sons of the South» who, at the end of the Sixties came to Milan, when still very young, to seek his fortune. The glittering windows of the metropolis were the stimulus for improvement, learning, and aiming upwards. Then came work experience in London and later the opportunity to prove himself in competitions, meetings and international events.

The idea of a school for gourmet pastry-making must have some impetus, and the story of *Cast Alimenti* is inextricably linked to Santoro. Since then Vittorio has had to forget the limelight of his own workshop and devote himself to improving a sector that has always required great professionalism and preparation. As the school's director, Vittorio passes on his commitment and passion. «In this profession you cannot rely on intuition or on momentary brilliance. You need a basic training, continuing education, scientific knowledge of food and only then will customers come to appreciate our achievements».

SOFT AND CRUNCHY IN A GLASS (P. 140)

CAST ALIMENTI

Via Serenissima 5, Brescia
tel. +39.030.2350076
www.castalimenti.it

BARBARA AND DAVIDE SCABIN
GENIUS AND MODERATION

These two are like the owl and the lark. He is the genius of the nightlife; she is the fresh spirit of daytime continuity, tireless supporter of her brother in a flavor factory in the shadow of a castle touched by the magic of contemporary art. There could be no better place for Davide and Barbara Scabin, the soul and engine of a restaurant that has been called a fair-ground for gourmets, where "cooking projects" are tried out. It is not a contradiction: Davide Scabin argues that a large kitchen staff must organize the work in ingenious and precise ways to give continuity to creativity.

Davide designs and Barbara organizes. Davide invents and Barbara executes. Davide has studied in a hoteliers' school and then participated in various work-study experiences all around Europe. Barbara attended the Art Institute, and was soon co-opted into her brother's venture. Davide is the genius, Barbara is moderation. They explain: «Designing a dish is not an aesthetic form for us; it relates to the conception of that proposal. And before the dish leaves the kitchen, we look at it, seated at a table, "reading" it with precisely the same mind as that of the customer».

The career of Davide Scabin began in 1993 in a restaurant in Almese, a town on the outskirts of Turin going toward the Alps, called *Al Combal. Punto Zero*, from 2002, is its natural evolution. But his «first time in the kitchen» was in 1980 in Fiano in the Turin area. Today in that parallelepipedon next to the Castello del Rivoli, anything can happen: a 14-course tasting menu with surprising dishes, from «cyber egg» to «*Matrioska di Tropea* (onion)», a traditional dinner with agnolotti and veal with tuna sauce, an event for a hundred people. «In my restaurant, it is forbidden to say this dish came out well. One says: «This is how I made it». Genius or moderation?

TOAST WITH NUTELLA AND TOMATO (MÈC COMBAL) P. 142

COMBAL.ZERO
Piazza Mafalda di Savoia – Castello di Rivoli, Rivoli (To)
tel. +39.011.9565225
www.combalzero.it

EMANUELE SCARELLO
ALWAYS AMONG FRIENDS

In June, the duty on wheat increased from 1.40 to 3 lira per quintal; in August, Francesco Crispi took over as president of the Council; in December the Triple Alliance was formed between Italy, England and Austria. In Godia, a ward of Udine near Carnia, the Italians had just arrived, after the Austro-Hungarians. It was 1887. In the resale of food one speaks Furlan, as always. «My great-grandfather was given a license as a golden handshake from the King». Then the tavern was set up in 1920. «Later my father Tino and my mother Ivonne decided to transform the bar and open the restaurant *Agli Amici*». It was 1963.

Emanuele Scarello was born eight years later. With the help of his sister Michela, the old restaurant was transformed. After hoteliers' school, Emanuele went to Spain, Austria, France, then in 1997, with him cooking and her serving in the dining room, they took over the family business. Then came the French star in 2000, the place became an elegant restaurant and in 2009 Scarello was elected president of the Italian JRE, the *Jeunes Restaurateurs d'Europe*.

«For some weeks we had here, doing an internship, a young man who worked for Tony May in New York. One morning, following my trip to the mill for hand-ground flour, and to a dairy farm to look for ricotta, he looked at me with some surprise and asked me: "Excuse me, but where is the business?" For me, it's this: waking up every morning to look for something good to cook». Despite the pyrotechnic inventions with jellies, cold-warm contrasts, surprises in the dish, *Agli Amici* does not forget the products of its "lucky land", halfway between sea, plain and mountain, interpreted with humorous, cheerful and playful creativity. With the same hospitality since 1887.

NUTELLA WITH BREAD STICKS (P. 144)

AGLI AMICI
Via Liguria 250, Fr. Godia, Udine
tel. +39.0432.565411
www.agliamici.it

MAURO ULIASSI
FALLING IN LOVE ON THE EAST WHARF

The elegant lady at the table tastes the dish of yellowtail with creamed sea urchin. It is an explosion of pure sea. She bites the little thing and can't stop herself from saying to her husband: «But this is positively orgasmic». He looks at her, embarrassed: «Yes, dear, I heard the waves against the cliff». It can happen at the tables on the East wharf of Senigallia, where, in the kitchen, you will find a smooth, dark-eyed type. A Charles Aznavour type, with a head of unruly curls and a Marche accent.

Mauro Uliassi chose to be a cook out of love, when he already had a ticket in his pocket for Paris, where the great Pierre Hermé was waiting for him to go and work with him at *Fauchon*. It was 1983, and Mauro was the type who liked discothèques, sidecars, and the beach. He earned well in the restaurants of the Adriatic coast, with fried and grilled fish, and studied sociology at the University. Then he met a female sociologist: better than a male sociologist any day. «It was love at first sight». He fell in love and prepared to win her over with a sort of *Babette's Feast* that entailed two days of work. Result: the sociologist became his wife and a few years later, in 1990, he opened the restaurant Uliassi, which has made him internationally famous. Not with his wife, who continues to practice sociology, but with his sister Katia serving in the dining room. He confirms it: «I cook because I'm in love. I am in love with the people who come to me; I want to win them over with my creations, thanks to a staff that can think, work and act like a great orchestra. Indeed, I would say that the chef is just the tip of the iceberg...». A dinner at the *Banchina di Levante*, you can be sure, is always love at first taste.

WAFER OF DUCK FOIE GRAS AND NUTELLA WITH A SHOT OF KIR ROYAL (P. 146)

ULIASSI CUCINA DI MARE
Banchina di Levante 6, Senigallia (An)
tel. +39.071.65463
www.uliassi.it

LUISA VALAZZA
AND THE STARS SHONE

Although she has been cooking for almost thirty years, ever since she was young, she has never put aside the desire to experiment, to stay in the game, to try out new experiences. It might be because she travels a lot, because she is invited to represent Italian cuisine all over the world. It might be because in her charming restaurant everything works well, thanks to the professionalism of her husband Angelo. It might be that the presence of her daughter Paola bodes well for the continuity of the restaurant, but Luisa Valazza is always in a good mood, despite all the hard work and fatigue in a profession that has never given particularly good media coverage to

women. For Luisa, who from time to time has been called the professor of cooking, the queen of the restaurant business, the menu artist, creating a special dish is a moment of joy.

We are in Novara, in northern Piedmont, in a quiet village where you find this outpost of the Relais & Châteaux circuit, one of the most famous in Italy since the end of the Nineties when the restaurant was awarded the coveted third Michelin star. As the grand dame of Italian cuisine, Luisa Valazza insists on defending the true tradition: «Now Italian products can be found everywhere abroad, while once they were more difficult to find, but few know how to use them...».

In a time of great change, and the pursuit of fashions and trends, at *Sorriso* in Soriso the focus is on refinement: rice with pumpkin and amaretto, red mullet and Jerusalem artichoke, fillet of venison with apple. It was 1981 when that girl, a graduate in literature, and that gentleman, opened their restaurant, a long-desired dream of love: Tosca's stars continue to shine.

BONBON OF DUCK LIVER, HAZELNUTS AND NUTELLA WITH PEACHES AND SOFT RECIOTO WINE JELLY (P. 148)

AL SORRISO

Via Roma 18, Soriso (No)
tel. +39.0322.983228
www.alsorriso.com

ILARIO VINCIGUERRA
FRAGRANCES TO SAVOR

The instructions to taste the dish that opens the sarabande of surprises and pleasures are given by Marika, who handles hospitality with great professionalism: «You must open the plexiglass sphere and smell the aroma of fresh shrimp from Mazzara del Vallo and extra virgin olive oil. Then you must close it and shake it to mix the other ingredients, edible flowers and jellies with Sorrento lemons and squid ink. The base of ice, gin and tonic give it a final note of alcohol». And what about Neapolitan wheat and ricotta cake served on a spoon with a biscuit and a spherical treatment?

We are on the shores of Lake Varese, in a small town where the *Antica Trattoria Monte Costone* was once located. Here, since July 2000, everything has changed, with the young and talented chef Ilario Vinciguerra, born 1975, who with his wife Marika serving in the dining room, has given an innovative flair to the menu of this cozy restaurant. That opening dish earned him a major award at the Spanish exhibition *Lo Mejor de la Gastronomia*, in 2007; it is called *Profumo* and is one of the mainstays of the restaurant's menu.

Ilario explains it bluntly: «Cooking should be fun, provide sensations, bring a feeling to the dish. I wish my menu was recognizable even with closed eyes». But then he has always forged his way looking for something new: a Neapolitan through and through, after hoteliers' school in Formia he worked in several starred restaurants in France, including Ducasse's *Louis XV* in Montecarlo, and the *Residence de la Pinede* in St Tropez, in Germany, in Switzerland, and in Belgium, before returning to Italy to *Don Alfonso* on the Amalfi Coast. Today his sous-chef is Japanese: the contaminations continue.

STRAWBERRY-CHOC (P. 150)

ILARIO VINCIGUERRA RESTAURANT

Via IV Novembre 10, Galliate Lombardo (Va)
tel. +39.0332.947104
www.ilariovinciguerra.it

JONATHAN WAXMAN
THE LUXURY OF SIMPLICITY

Regarded as one of "America's most influential people" of the last year by «Esquire»" magazine, Jonathan Waxman has helped to create the New American Cuisine, with intelligence, irony, all-European know-how and a passion for Italy. His dishes are simple and fresh, with a rich flavor. And they were already so in the mid-Eighties, when Jonathan, having arrived from the West Coast after experiencing the creations of Alice Waters at *Chez Panisse*, introduced New Yorkers to the legendary California cuisine at his restaurant *Jams*.

His fate was not to be a chef. As he recounted in his first book, *A Great American Cook*, published in 2007, he was supposed to have become a professional trombone player, after having founded a rock band at Berkeley, and graduating. It was a trip to France in 1977 that allowed him to discover the Troigros brothers' nouvelle cuisine, in addition to La Varenne's school in Paris. It was the turning point: fresh ingredients in season, few condiments, and simpler dishes.

In his restaurants, Waxman has trained dozens of chefs whose careers have then taken off: in 2002 he opened *Washington Park*, followed two years later by the Italian-style bistro *Barbuto*, housed in a former garage in the West Village, which in summer is completely open, like an outdoor Parisian café. The menu is casual and rustic, and almost all in Italian: paccheri bolognese, manzo ai ferri, frutti di bosco con brodo. He explains his philosophy of cooking like this: «I like crunch in the bread, spice in the sauce, and crispness in the filling».

PIZZA S'MORE (P. 152)

BARBUTO
775 Washington Street (West 12th Street), New York, NY
tel. +1 212.924.9700
www.barbutonyc.com

ANDREA ZANIN
FEELINGS IN THE FORM OF ZALETI

Venice is not just the all-consuming city of Thomas Mann and Giuseppe Berto, it is also home to the *mercadanti*, the merchants and their trade, to the eighteenth-century traditions of the world's most famous carnival and the sweet dishes that you can find down the lanes and in the squares: *bussolai*, *zaleti*, *pinza* and *fritöe*. It is in this vital and joyful vein that we associate one of the best-known figures in Venetian pastry making, representative of a family which, in Mestre, since 1967, is synonymous with sweetness, and has now conquered the entire lagoon. Andrea Zanin is its undisputed "doge", a man who has forged his way past many milestones since 1986, when he took over the business. Today his most prestigious achievement is that of becoming a member – one of the few in Italy – of the international association Relais Dessert. For years he has been a driving force with the Academy of Italian Master Pastry Chefs and has won numerous awards.

Zanin is a man of good humor, open and cheerful, with an infectious laugh. A friend to all. He is satisfied, as a Venetian *mercadante*, with what he has managed to achieve with his work. But he is not a businessman without a soul: «When you work 15-16 hours a day, like me, you can't do it without having a great passion. My joy comes from the possibility of conveying feelings through my flavors».

There are more and more cooks who become pastry chefs, or vice versa. «When I cook, I do it with the same precision that I dedicate to pastry making». But zaleti, the traditional Venetian pastries made with corn flour, are better in his opinion. This, however, Andrea does not say aloud, but rather with those smiling eyes that you only find in someone as sweet as him.

DOLCE DOGE (P. 154)

PASTICCERIA ZANIN
Via Bissuola 24, Mestre-Venezia
tel. +39.041.5343262
Other shops: Mestre, Treviso, Dubai, Abu Dhabi
www.andreazanin.it

LUCA ZECCHIN
HILLS SERVED UP ON A PLATE

Fifty years separated them. A common passion united them. She was born in 1930. He was born in 1980. She had the hands of a grandmother who could create dishes imbued with the traditions of the hills of the Langhe and Monferrato. He has the eyes of a boy who learns quickly. Together, for years, they represented the extraordinary cuisine of the restaurant *Guido da Costigliole*. Following the death of Lidia Alciati (page 209), Luca Zecchin remained at the Relais San Maurizio, holding the memory of her high in the minds of all.

After hoteliers' school at Agliano Terme (AT), Luca gained experience in other restaurants, and then at the age of twenty, in 2000, went to work in the restaurant run by mamma Lidia. «Now I feel a little bit part of the family, after so many years...» admits the chef, smiling, now that he has also gone into partnership with the Alciati family.

If in the early years, Luca Zecchin sought innovation with ingenious dishes like *abbiamo fritto l'uovo* (we fried the egg), thereby offsetting tradition by creating one of the most interesting menus in Piedmont, he is now going through a phase of reflection, which has brought him closer to the hills around the *Relais San Maurizio*, citing some of Lidia's famous dishes though with some changes, such as salt cod with potatoes and porcini mushrooms. This is Luca's philosophy: «We are all tired, in Italy, of fake cuisine. For this reason, I've put chicken cacciatore back on the menu: you have to return to the flavors of yesteryear. However, you never stop learning, with the eyes even before than with the palate. When I have a day off, even now that I have a staff of seven, I go out and try my colleagues' specialties. At times "I see" the dishes, I imagine them while I'm lying in bed, and then maybe one will suddenly come into creation».

CREAMY RISOTTO WITH PUMPKIN AND NUTELLA (P. 156)

RELAIS SAN MAURIZIO GUIDO DA COSTIGLIOLE
Loc. San maurizio, Santo Stefano Belbo (Cn)
tel. +39.0141.841900
www.relaissanmaurizio.it

APPENDIX

BIBLIOGRAPHY

Barthes R. – *Miti d'oggi*, Einaudi, Torino 1974

Bertola R. – *Jo Condor*, Sei, Torino 1976

Bragaglia C. – *Sequenze di gola*, Cadmo, Milano 2002

Campanelli C., Taurino M. – *NG bicchieri promozionali*, Centrostampa, Roma 2000

Casella C. – *True Tuscan*, Harper Collins, New York 2005

Cassini R. – *Il piccolo libro della Nutella*, Mondadori, Milano 2000

Cassini R. – *Nutella Nutellae*, Liber Magno, Comix, Modena 1995

Cassini R. – *Nutella 2 La vendetta*, Comix Pillole, Modena 1994

Cirio R. – *Qualità, scénes d'objets à l'italienne*, Editions du May, Paris 1990

Ciuffoletti Z. (ed.) – *Dolceamaro*, Alinari, Firenze 2003

Culicchia G. – *Tutti giù per terra*, Tea, Milano 1999

Culicchia G. – *Brucia la città*, Mondadori, Milano, 2009

De Vecchi S., Di Nola A., Tonelli M. – *Storia di un successo*, Aeda, Torino 1967

Fabris G., Padovani G. – *Nutella siamo noi*, not for public sale, Ferrero Spa, Pino Torinese 1996

Farinetti G. – *L'isola che brucia*, Marsilio, Venezia 1997

Fo J. – *Ti amo ma il tuo braccio destro mi fa schifo, tagliatelo*, Oscar Mondadori, Milano 2000

Giusti G. – *Il grande libro di Carosello*, Sperling & Kupfer, Milano 1995

Grasso A. (ed.) – *Enciclopedia della televisione*, Garzanti, Milano 1996

Guarnaschelli Gotti M. (ed.) – *Grande enciclopedia illustrata della gastronomia*, Mondadori, Milano 2007

Iacchetti G. (ed.) – *Italianità*, Corraini, Mantova, 2009

Kostioukovitch E. – *Perché agli italiani piace parlare del cibo*, Sperling & Kupfer, Milano, 2006

Lévy J. – *Incontro*, Frassinelli, Milano 1996

Marelli M. – *La fisica del tacco 12*, Rizzoli, Milano, 2009

Mariani J.F. – *The Dictionary of American Food and Drink*, Hearst Books, New York 1994

McLuhan M. – *Understanding Media: The Extensions of Man*, McGraw Hill, New York 1964

Mazzantini M. – *Venuto al mondo*, Mondadori, Milano, 2008

Mondadori S. – *Un anno fa domani*, Instar, Torino, 2009

Oggero M. – *L'amica americana*, Mondadori, Milano, 2005

Padovani G. – *Gnam! Storia sociale della Nutella*, Castelvecchi, Roma 1999

Padovani G. – *Nutella, un mito italiano*, Rizzoli, Milano, 2004

Pigna A. – *Miliardari in borghese*, Mursia, Milano 1966

Rodotà M.L. – *Pizza di farro alla rucola con Nutella e altre stranezze italiane*, Sperling & Kupfer, Milano 1995

Various authors – *Cento anni di prodotto italiano (exhibition catalogue)*, Parco Scientifico e Tecnologico Galileo, Padova 2002

Various authors – *Ferrero 1946-1996*, not for public sale, Ferrero Spa, Pino Torinese 1996

Volo F. – *Esco a fare due passi*, Mondadori, Milano, 2001

Waxman J. – *A Great American Cook*, Houghton Mifflin Company, Boston New York 2007

INDEX OF CHEFS' RECIPES BY COURSE

RECIPE INDEX IN ALPHABETICAL ORDER

ICONOGRAPHICAL REFERENCES

ACKNOWLEDGEMENTS

My first heartfelt thanks go to the 40 chefs and pastry cooks who have given me their time, their ideas and their images: they were all invaluable, congenial, devoted and affectionate travelling companions during work on the first edition of this book in 2006 and have been again for this second edition.

Sincere thanks go to my friend and writer Andrea Lee for her ironic and stimulating preface.

I am also grateful to the artists Eugenio Comencini and Silvano Costanzo for the works of art reproduced in this book.

For the photographs in the «Chefs' Nutella» section, I thank Francesca Brambilla and Serena Serrani.

For the section "The Scent of Home" I received a professional contribution from Rosalba Gioffré.

My personal thanks go to Giada Riondino for her efforts in completing this project.

I also wish to thank the Ferrero Spa group for their cooperation in the search for archive data and business images. The book however comes from an idea of my own, shared by my husband Gigi Padovani.

Special thanks go to the following people who contributed to the realization of this project:
Pio Boffa, Marco Brambilla, Sarah Branduardi, Antonio Castiglia, Lorenza Cerbini, Chiara Del Cogliano, Alessia Gorni, Karl W. Krohn, Maurizio Molinari, Sabrina Notarnicola, Pier Aldo Oldano, Maria Risi, Sara Rosso, Francine Segan, Francesco Semprini, Daniele Solavaggione, Cenk Sonmezsoy, Mario Strola, Raoul Romoli Venturi.

Further thanks are due to the following institutions and organizations that generously contributed information and images:
Documentation Center of «La Stampa»; «Le Carrousel du Louvre»; Palazzo dei Diamanti di Ferrara; Mistiche Nutella; Italian School Of Design in Padua; Studio Nadadora, Valencia; Ballarini Paolo & Figli spa, Rivarolo Mantovano; Agence Patrick Jouin, Paris; Corraini Publisher.

Clara Vada Padovani
Turin, July 2010

passione Nutella | Appendix